# DOCTRINE, JUDGMENT, AND MORAL ORDER

## *Doctrine of Evil, Corruption, Judgment, and Covenant Order*

### MBRS Book 2 — Bachelor-Level Formation

### The Official Student Textbook

DR. YERAL E. OGANDO

# DOCTRINE, JUDGMENT, AND MORAL ORDER

## The Official Student Textbook for the Master of Biblical Restoration Studies (MBRS)
### By
### Dr. Yeral E. Ogando

Authored and published by
Dr. Yeral E. Ogando
Adopted for instructional use by
Yahuah Institute of Biblical Restoration, Inc.
As the core text for
The Master of Biblical Restoration Studies (MBRS) Program

Scripture quotations are taken exclusively from Dabar Yahuah Scriptures – www.yahuahbible.com. This textbook is produced for academic, instructional, and theological training purposes within the MBRS program and affiliated courses.
"All instructional texts used by the MBRS Program are independently authored and published by Dr. Yeral E. Ogando. The Institute adopts these texts solely for instructional purposes and does not own, publish, or receive revenue from them."

ISBN: 978-1-946249-47-0

# 1. AUTHORIZATION & INSTITUTIONAL STATEMENT

This textbook, Foundations of Biblical Restoration, is authored and published by Dr. Yeral E. Ogando and is adopted and approved for instructional use by Yahuah Institute of Biblical Restoration, Inc. as the core instructional text for the Master of Biblical Restoration Studies (MBRS) program.

All doctrinal positions, terminology, instructional structures, and evaluative standards contained within this volume are governed exclusively by Dabar Yahuah Scriptures as preserved in the Scriptures recognized by the Institute: the inspired writings of the Tanakh (Old Testament), the preserved Apokryfos, and the Renewed Covenant (New Testament) writings.

This text operates within a closed canonical and theological framework for the academic cycle in which it is issued. No external denominational systems, philosophical methodologies, speculative Yada Yahuah (theology), or institutional traditions are permitted to govern interpretation, instruction, or assessment within the MBRS program.

This Student Edition is authorized for instructional use solely within the MBRS program.

Unauthorized reproduction, distribution, or use outside of Institute-approved instructional contexts is prohibited.

# 2. PREFACE & STATEMENT OF PURPOSE

Foundations of Biblical Restoration exists because Scripture itself demands restoration.

This textbook was not written to defend denominational systems, preserve inherited theology, or harmonize philosophical frameworks with Scripture. It was written to allow **Dabar Yahuah** to govern Yada Yahuah (theology) without competition.

Modern theology often begins with assumptions and searches Scripture for support. Restoration Yada Yahuah (theology) reverses that order. Scripture establishes authority, defines categories, diagnoses corruption, and reveals restoration according to divine intent rather than human tradition.

This book serves as the **single, integrated instructional text** for the Master of Biblical Restoration Studies (MBRS). It guides the student from Scriptural Witness through, *Yahuah: Restoration Guide,* the ***Origin of Evil:*** *Biblical Truths Hidden in Plain Sight,* the **Three Humanities™**: *The Division of Humanity in Yahuah's Plan* - Volume 1, and th*e **Three Humanities™**: The Restoration of the First Humanity in Yahuah's Plan*—culminating in independent thesis defense.

## 3. STATEMENT OF PURPOSE

The purpose of this textbook is to:

    Establish Scripture as the sole governing authority

    Restore biblical categories obscured by tradition and translation

    Define evil without attributing corruption to Yahuah

    Explain humanity through the **Three Humanities™** framework

    Present restoration as transformation, not repair

    Prepare students to defend **Restoration Yada Yahuah** (theology)

independently and accurately

This text is not devotional. It is not speculative. It is instructional, corrective, and authoritative.

## 4. PROGRAM LEARNING OUTCOMES
### MASTER OF BIBLICAL RESTORATION STUDIES (MBRS)

Upon successful completion of the MBRS program, the student will be able to:

**1.Demonstrate Covenantal Reasoning** across the full body of Scripture, integrating the Tanakh (Old Testament), Apokryfos, and Renewed Covenant (New Testament) writings without contradiction.

**2.Explain Scriptural authority** as divinely originated, canonically bounded, and covenantal preserved.

**3.Define evil, corruption, judgment, and restoration** using Scriptural categories alone, without reliance on philosophical or denominational frameworks.

**4.Articulate the Three Humanities™ framework** (First, Second, Third Humanities and the Variant) using Scripture-governed anthropology and lineage Yada Yahuah (theology).

**5.Distinguish between sin, corruption, and Creational alteration**, explaining why restoration requires transformation rather than moral repair.

**6.Apply covenant language discipline responsibly,** demonstrating how words govern doctrine and prevent theological distortion.

**7.Defend Restoration Yada Yahuah (theology)** from creation to consummation as a unified, Scripture-consistent system.

**8.Produce and defend a master-level thesis** grounded exclusively in Scripture, demonstrating doctrinal clarity, canonical consistency, and methodological integrity.

## 5. HOW TO USE THIS TEXTBOOK

This textbook is designed for **structured, sequential use** within the MBRS program.

### STUDENT RESPONSIBILITIES

- Read all assigned Scripture before engaging commentary or explanations.
- Follow the progression of weeks and months without skipping sections.
- Use only Institute-approved Scriptural sources when completing assignments.

- Adhere strictly to locked templates, prompts, and evaluation criteria.
- Demonstrate mastery through clarity, Scripture use, and disciplined reasoning.

## INSTRUCTIONAL STRUCTURE

- Each Term builds upon previous authority and doctrine.
- Each Month introduces defined instructional goals.
- Each Week focuses on specific Scriptural concepts.
- Assessments measure integration and reasoning, not memorization.

This text is not designed for casual reading.
It is designed for **formation, correction, and qualification.**

*Students who attempt to bypass structure, introduce external systems, or rely on speculation will not advance.*

# 6. ACADEMIC & SCRIPTURAL INTEGRITY STATEMENT

Enrollment in the MBRS program constitutes agreement to the following standards:
- **Scripture governs all conclusions.**
- **Dabar Yahuah is the highest authority.**
- No denominational, philosophical, or speculative systems may override Scripture.
- All work must be original, truthful, and accurately cited.
- Plagiarism, doctrinal innovation, or misrepresentation of Scripture results in disqualification.
- Advancement is evaluative, not automatic.

This program values **clarity over creativity**, **submission over speculation, and truth over tradition.**

The goal is not affirmation, but formation.

**Authorized Textual Resources and Access**

The instructional texts and Scriptural resources referenced within the Master of Biblical Restoration Studies (MBRS) program are made available through designated platforms.

Primary reference texts and supporting source materials authored by Dr. Yeral E. Ogando are openly accessible at www.yahuahdabar.com. These materials may be read online by any visitor. Registration allows users to download PDF versions of the source texts. These materials are publicly available and are not restricted to enrolled students.

The Dabar Yahuah Scriptures, including the Tanakh (Old Testament), Apokryfos, and Renewed Covenant (New Testament) writings, are openly accessible for online reading at www.yahuahbible.com. These texts are provided as the authorized Scriptural reference for the MBRS program and are available to all readers.

For Scriptural study and term-level consultation, students are instructed to use the Dabar Yahuah Scriptures App, including its Strong Concordance tools for Hebrew and Greek reference. This tool is used for confirming word forms, meanings, and Scriptural usage in alignment with the Institute's instructional framework.

The Student Edition textbooks, however, are not publicly distributed through these websites. Student textbooks are provided through the Institute's instructional platform or authorized course distribution channels, with the exception of the Amazon print edition.

These access distinctions are intentional and form part of the Institute's instructional and evaluative framework.

# Contents

# TERM II — DOCTRINE, JUDGMENT, AND MORAL ORDER
## STAGE II OF THE MASTER-LEVEL PROGRAM (ECCLESIASTICAL)

Bachelor-Level Formation · Months 5–8

## ACADEMIC ORIENTATION — TERM II · MONTH 1

Term II marks the formal transition into Bachelor-level Yada Yahuah study within the Master-level program of the Yahuah Institute of Biblical Restoration, Inc. This stage assumes successful completion of all Term I coursework (Associate-Level Foundations) and demonstrated mastery of Scriptural Witness, preservation, covenant continuity, and restored Yada' Yahuah methodology. At this level, students are expected to reason from Scripture with increased analytical precision, terminological discipline, and covenantal coherence. Interpretive leniency is reduced. Unsupported assumptions, inherited Yada Yahuah frameworks, and speculative abstractions are no longer tolerated. Month 1 establishes non-negotiable doctrinal boundaries that govern all subsequent study of evil, corruption, judgment, redemption, and restoration. These boundaries are derived from Scripture itself and must be applied consistently throughout Term II.

Students must demonstrate the ability to suspend inherited Yada Yahuah assumptions and allow Scripture to define its own categories, agents, and moral distinctions.

## STUDENTS ARE EXPECTED TO:

Preserve the character of Yahuah as morally pure and without corruption
Distinguish definition from consequence, and judgment from moral evil
Trace causation using Scriptural logic rather than philosophical abstraction
Handle language, translation, and agency with disciplined care

Failure to master Month 1 will compromise all subsequent doctrinal reasoning in Term II and will require remediation before advancement.

# TERM II · MONTH 1
MODULE OVERVIEW
Defining Evil According to Scripture Alone
(The Origin of Evil: Biblical Truths Hidden in Plain Sight — Chapters 1–4)

This module begins Term II, which is entirely dedicated to the study of The Origin of Evil using Scripture as the sole authority. Month 1 establishes the foundational definitions without which all later discussion becomes distorted. This month teaches students how Scripture itself defines evil, what evil is not, and why evil cannot be attributed to Yahuah. Students will learn to abandon philosophical assumptions, cultural narratives, and inherited Yada Yahuah traditions, and instead allow Scripture to define its own categories.

By the end of this month, the student will understand that:
- Evil is not created by Yahuah
- Evil is not synonymous with judgment
- Evil is not a necessary counterpart to good
- Evil arises through rebellion and corruption
- Translation and language often blur Scriptural clarity

This month lays the non-negotiable foundation for all future discussion on sin, corruption, judgment, redemption, and restoration.

## Methodological Continuity — Scriptural Definition & Preservation of Divine Character

This module continues the restorative, Scripture-first methodology established in Term I and hardened for Bachelor-level rigor. All material in Month 1 is governed by the following principles:
- Scripture Defines Its Own Categories
  Evil, judgment, corruption, and agency must be defined by Scriptural usage, not philosophical or cultural constructs.
- The Character of Yahuah Is the Fixed Reference Point

- Any Yada Yahuah conclusion that compromises Yahuah's righteousness, justice, or purity is rejected as invalid.
  Causation Must Be Traced, Not Assumed
- Evil must be followed from origin to manifestation using Scriptural logic, not abstract speculation.
  Language and Translation Require Discipline
- Hebrew and Greek terms must be examined contextually to prevent false Yada Yahuah conclusions.

These principles govern all readings, study tasks, and assessments in Term II · Month 1.

## *MODULE LEARNING OUTCOMES — TERM II · MONTH 1*
## BY THE END OF TERM II · MONTH 1, STUDENTS SHOULD BE ABLE TO:

Define evil exclusively using Scriptural categories

Demonstrate from Scripture that evil does not originate in Yahuah

Distinguish moral evil from judgment, calamity, and consequence

Explain the relationship between rebellion, corruption, and evil

Apply covenant language discipline to passages commonly mistranslated as attributing evil to Yahuah

Preserve the character of Yahuah as the foundation of all doctrinal reasoning

Mastery is demonstrated through accurate Scriptural citation, logical coherence, and disciplined category preservation.

### CHAPTER COVERAGE
- The Origin of Evil — Chapters 1–4
- Chapter 1 — What Evil Is Not
- Chapter 2 — The Character of Yahuah
- Chapter 3 — Sin vs. Corruption
- Chapter 4 — Words for Evil

*TERM II · MONTH 1 — WEEK 17*
# ORDER BEFORE CORRUPTION
Creation, Assignment, and the First Deception

## Week 17 Learning Outcomes — Created Order and Historical Sequence

By the end of Week 17, students should be able to trace the structure of creation as presented in Scripture and Second Temple witnesses, distinguishing between eternal and mortal beings according to assigned function rather than value. Students should be able to explain why angels do not procreate while humanity does, identify deception as the first historical mechanism through which disobedience is introduced, and distinguish clearly between the knowledge of evil and the creation of evil. Finally, students should demonstrate how corruption enters history progressively rather than instantaneously and articulate how divine order preserves the righteousness of Yahuah without philosophical defense or speculation.

## Purpose of Week 17

Week 17 establishes **order as the prerequisite for understanding** corruption. Before Scripture addresses rebellion, violence, or judgment, it first reveals how creation was structured, how roles were assigned, and how boundaries were established. Evil is not introduced as a rival power, a created substance, or an internal flaw within Yahuah's work. Instead, Scripture presents evil as a **historical intrusion** that enters an already ordered reality through deception and disobedience.

The purpose of this week is methodological. Students are trained to read Scripture sequentially and juridically, learning to identify **assignment before violation, structure before collapse, and function before corruption.** Without this discipline, later discussions of Watchers, hybridization, judgment, and preservation inevitably collapse into accusation against Yahuah. Week 17 therefore safeguards divine righteousness by teaching students to reason from order rather than emotion, tradition, or philosophical assumption.

**Term II · Month 1 · Week 17 — Reading**

Read Chapter 1 from The Origin of Evil: Biblical Truths Hidden in Plain Sight
The Scriptural witnesses below are not presented to retell the chapter, but to train students in how Chapter 1 must be read.

## CREATION OF ALL SPIRITS — THE FIRST DAY

- **Yôbêl (Jubilees) 2:2–3**

   This passage establishes the **priority of the invisible realm**. Students must note that Scripture places the creation of all spirits—including angelic beings and the spirits of humanity—at the beginning of creation, before the visible order is completed. This ordering is essential: history unfolds from an already-constituted spiritual framework.

- **Chănôk (Enoch) 15:6–7**

   These verses clarify assignment, not value. Angelic beings are described as eternal and immortal, and for that reason are not appointed wives. Students must learn to read this not as deprivation, but as design: eternity excludes procreation by definition.

- **Yirmeyâhû (Jeremiah) 1:5 and Tehīllīm (Psalms) 139:13**

   These texts confirm that human spirits are known, sanctified, and purposed prior to embodiment, while bodily formation occurs later through divine craftsmanship. The student must observe that Scripture distinguishes spirit identity from bodily timing without confusion or contradiction.

Taken together, these witnesses establish a foundational principle for Term II: All spirits are created by Yahuah, but not all spirits are assigned the same function, duration, or mode of continuation.

## CREATION OF HUMANITY — THE SIXTH DAY

- **Yôbêl (Jubilees) 2:14–15**
  Students are to observe the distinction between **creation of humanity and human relational sequence.** Man is created on the sixth day as the first embodied human and is assigned dominion. The woman is also created on the sixth day as fully human, sharing the same nature and purpose.

- Their creation establishes sexual distinction and human continuity, not immediate relational union. Encounter, covenant, and companionship occur later within ordered sequence. This distinction is critical for avoiding Yada Yahuah confusion and anachronistic assumptions.

- **Chănôk (Enoch) 15:5**
  Procreation is presented as a compensatory gift granted to mortal beings so that nothing would be lacking on the earth. Mortality and reproduction are inseparable within divine order. Angels are eternal and therefore non-procreative; humans are mortal and therefore generative.

Students must learn to read difference without hierarchy. Function is not value. Angels serve; humanity continues creation through lineage.

## THE FIRST DECEPTION IN EDEN

- **Chănôk (Enoch) 69:6**
  This passage identifies Gadreel as the agent who led Chawwâh astray. The emphasis here is not character biography but agency: deception enters history through an acting being, not through Yahuah and not through creation itself.

- **Yôbêl (Jubilees) 3:17–19**
  The deception is carried out through suggestion rather than force. The Nâchâsh introduces doubt, reframes prohibition, and minimizes consequence. Students must observe that disobedience is not compelled; it is

chosen.

This distinction is foundational: deception does not create evil as a substance. It introduces disobedience, which results in the knowledge of evil. Evil is encountered through transgression, not manufactured by Yahuah.

## CONSEQUENCE WITHOUT CORRUPTION OF CREATION

- **Berēshīṯh (Genesis) 3:22–24**
  The expulsion from Eden demonstrates early judgment as restriction rather than destruction. Humanity is prevented from immortalizing disobedience, but creation itself remains intact.

Students must note that this response preserves order. Judgment at this stage functions as containment, not annihilation, and does not imply corruption of creation itself.

## THE FIRST MURDER AND HISTORICAL ESCALATION

- **Berēshīṯh (Genesis) 4:3–4 and Yôbêl (Jubilees) 4:2**
  The murder of Hebel by Qayin marks the first instance of human violence. Students must resist the temptation to universalize this event. Scripture presents it as escalation, not saturation. Evil appears, but corruption has not yet become systemic.

This distinction prepares students to later recognize when Scripture signals a qualitative shift from isolated sin to total corruption.

A World Without Demons or Fallen Watchers

At this stage of history, Scripture presents a world in which demons do not yet exist, Watchers have not fallen, hybrid beings are absent, and corruption has not overtaken creation systemically. Evil exists as knowledge and choice, not as an external dominating force.

This observation is essential for maintaining chronological and doctrinal clarity in Term II.

## THE FIRST INVOCATION OF THE NAME OF YAHUAH

- **Berēshīth (Genesis) 4:26**
  The invocation of Yahuah's Name emerges gradually within the lineage of Sheth through Enosh. Covenant awareness develops progressively rather than appearing fully formed at creation.

Students should note that Scripture consistently presents restoration, worship, and covenant knowledge as unfolding historically.

## TEACHING EXPLANATION

Week 17 teaches students how to read Scripture from order to disorder, not the reverse. Chapter 1 establishes that all spirits are created by Yahuah, but their roles differ by assignment. Eternity is given to angels; procreation is given to humanity. Deception enters history through an angelic agent, not through divine authorship and not through creation itself.

The knowledge of evil arises through disobedience, not through design. Corruption escalates gradually—from deception to disobedience, from disobedience to expulsion, and from expulsion to violence—without demons, fallen Watchers, or hybrid beings at this stage.

By preserving sequence and assignment, Scripture safeguards Yahuah's righteousness without philosophical defense. Evil is introduced, not authored. Disorder arises through rebellion, not intention.

### Alignment Focus — Chapter 1 (The Origin of Evil)
From Chapter 1, students must retain:
- Order precedes corruption
- All spirits are created but not equally assigned
- Angels are eternal and non-procreative
- Humans are mortal and procreative

- Deception is the first entry point of disobedience
- Knowledge of evil is not the creation of evil
- Corruption escalates historically
- Covenant awareness develops progressively

### Key Terms and Definitions (Week 17)
- **Order:** Divine structure, assignment, and boundary established at creation.
- **Eternity:** The assigned state of angelic beings, excluding procreation.
- **Procreation:** The gift uniquely granted to humanity to preserve life in mortality.
- **Deception:** The mechanism through which disobedience is introduced.
- **Knowledge of Evil:** Awareness gained through transgression, not divine creation.

# COVENANTAL STUDY TASK

*Pause your reading and complete the following before proceeding. Engage the Scriptural text directly.*

*Compare angelic and human assignment and explain why difference does not imply hierarchy.*

**Explain why deception, rather than creation, introduces corruption.**
**Identify which forms of evil are absent at this stage of history.**
**Articulate how order preserves Yahuah's righteousness without argument.**

## FINAL THOUGHTS — WEEK 17

Corruption enters history; it does not originate in creation.

## QUOTE REFLECTION

"When order is restored, accusation loses its power."

# REBELLION, BOUNDARY VIOLATION, AND THE CORRUPTION OF THE EARTH

The Watchers, the Oath, and the Collapse of Created Order

## WEEK 18 LEARNING OUTCOMES — REBELLION AND JURIDICAL TRANSGRESSION

- By the end of Week 18, students should be able to:
- Identify the Watchers as authorized emissaries sent to instruct humanity
- Define the Watchers' mandate and the single prohibition governing their assignment
- Explain how corruption originates through persuasion, oath, and willful transgression
- Analyze the covenant of Mount Hermon as a deliberate act of rebellion
- Trace the emergence of corruption from boundary violation to systemic violence
- Demonstrate that hybridization violates created order and assigned nature
- Explain why judgment becomes necessary and irreversible in response to Watcher rebellion

## PURPOSE OF WEEK 18

Week 18 trains the student to read rebellion as a legal breach of assignment, not as metaphor, formation, or accidental failure. The goal is not to retell the events of Chapter 2, but to learn how Scripture and the assigned witnesses present a consistent sequence:

*authorized presence → corrupt counsel → oath-bound defiance → unlawful union → corrupted fruit → judicial response.*

This week therefore establishes the vocabulary and reasoning needed for the remainder of Term II. If students cannot distinguish temptation from rebellion, or sin from corruption, later judgment texts will be misread and the character of Yahuah will be misrepresented. Week 18 is not an emotional chapter. It is an ordered record of transgression, consequence, and restraint.

Term II · Month 1 · Week 18 — Reading

Read Chapter 2 from The Origin of Evil: Biblical Truths Hidden in Plain Sight

Then engage the Scriptural witnesses below. Your task is not to summarize the chapter, but to extract the doctrinal categories the chapter requires.

## THE MISSION OF THE WATCHERS

- **Yôbêl (Jubilees) 4:15**

  Read this text to establish legal starting position: the Watchers are not introduced as rebels, but as emissaries within mandate. Your focus is to identify:

what they were sent to do (function), what authority they carried (status), and why their later transgression must be read as abandonment of assignment rather than ignorance.

This passage supplies the foundation for a key discipline of Term II: corruption begins when authorized beings misuse lawful access.

## INCITEMENT AND COUNSEL TOWARD TRANSGRESSION

- **Chănôk (Enoch) 69:4–5**

  This reading trains students to locate where rebellion begins: not with the act, but with counsel. As you read, track the following:

  the role of persuasion in initiating deviation, the difference between suggestion and coercion, how "evil counsel" functions as a gateway into boundary violation.

Students must learn to treat counsel as agency, not as background detail. In Scriptural reasoning, counsel establishes responsibility.

# THE COVENANT OF MOUNT HERMON

**Chănôk (Enoch) 6:3–6**
This text must be treated juridically. The oath is not "drama." It is a legal mechanism that establishes three realities:
1. knowledge of prohibition,
2. collective commitment, and
3. irreversible intent.

The interpretive discipline here is crucial: the oath does not create rebellion; it seals it. Students must therefore distinguish between temptation (prior stage) and consummated defiance (oath-bound stage).
Boundary Violation and the Corruption of Created Order

At this point in the sequence, the student must identify the boundary in question: the Watchers cross the single limit that preserves distinction between what is heavenly and what is human. The issue is not romance, myth, or symbolism; it is the seizure of a function not assigned to them.

**Reason with categories Scripture requires:**
- assignment versus seizure,
- lawful access versus unlawful intrusion,
- distinction versus mixture,
- fruit as evidence of nature.

The key master-level discipline is this: boundary violation is proven by outcome, not asserted by opinion.

**The Birth of Hybrids and the Spread of Corruption**
- **Chănôk (Enoch) 7:1–6; 15:8–12**
  These readings must be approached as doctrinal witnesses, not as narrative material. Students should track four doctrinal features the texts emphasize:

1. the emergence of an unlawful category (hybrid fruit),
2. violence as the measurable expression of corruption,
3. creation-wide spread (humanity, animals, ecosystems),
4. the continuity of corruption after death through disembodied spirits.

Students must be trained to read the text's logic: the fruit defines the category. The Nephilim are not presented as merely sinful humans; they are presented as a corrupting presence whose effect is total.

### Systemic Corruption and the Necessity of Judgment

- **Yôbêl (Jubilees) 7:22**

   This passage is not included to dramatize destruction but to establish a threshold principle: once corruption becomes systemic, it is no longer managed through ordinary discipline. Students must identify how the text describes corruption as:
   - expanding beyond individuals,
   - consuming communities,
   - overtaking the environment,
   - producing self-devouring violence.

The doctrinal aim is to grasp why judgment in Term II functions as containment and preservation, not emotional retaliation.

### Judicial Response and Final Sentence

- **Chănôk (Enoch) 12–15**

   These chapters are read to establish that judgment is not chaos. It is formal, declared, and enforced. Students should track the judicial markers:
   - emissary appointment (Chănôk's role),
   - denied intercession (why appeal is rejected),
   - severed access (loss of heavenly standing),
   - binding and restraint,
   - sentence upon unlawful fruit.

This section trains the student to articulate why mercy is not offered at every stage: the texts present a point where rebellion is completed and judgment becomes necessary to preserve what remains.

**Teaching Explanation**

Week 18 teaches the student how to read rebellion as a structured descent: authorized beings abandon assignment through counsel, bind themselves by oath, seize a prohibited function, and generate corrupt fruit that spreads beyond private sin into creation-wide collapse.

The central interpretive skill this week requires is juridical reasoning: students must learn to identify who acts, by what permission, through what mechanism, and with what result. Hybridization is not treated as mythic imagery but as the consequence of unlawful mixture—proof that boundaries exist, matter, and can be violated.

Judgment, therefore, is not introduced as arbitrary severity. It appears as the required response when corruption becomes systemic and preservation of creation requires restraint.

## ALIGNMENT FOCUS – CHAPTER 2 (THE ORIGIN OF EVIL)

From Chapter 2, students must extract and retain:

- The Watchers begin as authorized emissaries
- Rebellion begins with counsel and persuasion, not ignorance
- The oath marks deliberate commitment and irreversible intent
- Boundary violation is defined by seizure of prohibited function
- Hybrid fruit functions as evidence of unlawful mixture
- Corruption spreads systemically, not privately
- Judgment functions as containment once corruption reaches totality
- Intercession is denied after rebellion is consummated

Key Terms and Definitions (Week 18)

- **Watcher Angels:** Authorized emissaries sent to instruct humanity in judgment and uprightness.
- **Boundary Violation:** The willful crossing of an assigned limit with knowledge of prohibition.
- **Oath:** A binding declaration that seals intent and removes retreat from transgression.
- **Hybridization:** Unlawful mixture that produces corrupt fruit and violates divine assignment.
- **Judgment:** Divine containment of irreversible corruption through authoritative decree and restraint.

# COVENANTAL STUDY TASK

*Pause your reading and complete the following before proceeding. Engage the Scriptural text directly.*

- *Identify the Watchers' mandate and state the single boundary attached to their assignment*
- *Explain why "counsel" is treated as agency and accountability in the text.*
- *Demonstrate why the oath is juridically significant rather than symbolic.*
- *Trace the sequence from boundary violation to systemic corruption and then to judicial response.*

## FINAL THOUGHTS — WEEK 18

"Corruption begins when assignment is rejected and boundaries are crossed."

## QUOTE REFLECTION

"Judgment is not the origin of disorder; it is the response to it."

# TERM II · MONTH 1 — WEEK 19
## TOTAL CORRUPTION AND IMMINENT JUDGMENT
From Hybrid Violence to the Necessity of the Deluge


Week 19 Learning Outcomes — Corruption as a Historical Condition

By the end of Week 19, students should be able to analyze corruption as a historical and material condition rather than a moral abstraction, demonstrating why Scripture presents the Deluge as an unavoidable act of purification. Students must be able to identify the Nephilim as the agents through whom corruption spreads to all flesh, distinguish ordinary human sin from the corruption of flesh produced by hybrid lineage, and explain why judgment becomes compulsory once corruption reaches totality.


**Purpose of Week 19**

Week 19 addresses a critical interpretive failure common in Yada Yahuah: the collapse of corruption into human moral weakness.

Chapter 3 does not describe a sinful society in need of reform; it describes a created order that has been structurally compromised.

This week trains students to recognize when Scripture shifts from addressing behavior to addressing condition, and from correction to removal. Without this distinction, the Deluge is misread as divine overreaction rather than judicial necessity.


Read Chapter 3 from **The Origin of Evil: Biblical Truths Hidden in Plain Sight**
(Fallen humanity, corrupted earth, imminent judgment)


## TERM II - MONTH 1 - WEEK 19 - READING
**Corruption as a Condition, Not an Accumulation of Sins**


Chapter 3 presents corruption as a state affecting all flesh.

The language of *"corrupted its way"* and *"corrupted their orders"* signals a breakdown of created distinctions, not merely ethical failure.

Students must observe that Scripture attributes this condition to the spread of Nephilim activity. The imagination described as "continually evil" is not presented as native to unaltered humanity, but as the consequence of hybrid domination over creation.

When Scripture speaks of *all flesh,* context determines whether moral agency or biological condition is in view. In Chapter 3, the emphasis is clearly the latter.

## The Nephilim as Agents of Systemic Collapse

Chapter 3 consistently identifies hybrid beings as the mechanism through which corruption expands:

- They devour humanity
- They corrupt animals and ecosystems
- They spread violence horizontally and vertically
- They exhaust creation itself

This is not metaphorical language. It describes material devastation that renders restoration impossible.

Students must resist importing later Yada Yahuah assumptions that flatten this into "human wickedness." Chapter 3 assigns responsibility precisely.

Nôach as Preservation, Not Moral Exception

The birth narrative of Nôach functions as a marker of continuity, not moral comparison.

Scripture emphasizes distinction, preservation, and separation rather than virtue signaling.

## Nôach represents:

- Uncorrupted human lineage
- Continuity of original creation
- Viability for covenant continuation

The text does not argue that Nôach is spared because others are morally worse, but because something remains that can still be preserved.

## Judgment as Purification, Not Punishment

Chapter 3 explicitly frames the Deluge as response to irreversible contamination.

## Key interpretive rule established here:

Judgment escalates in response to the degree of corruption, not the number of sins committed.

Once corruption consumes flesh, ecosystems, and lineage, forgiveness is no longer sufficient. Removal becomes the only means of preserving creation itself.

## Teaching Explanation

Week 19 establishes the decisive shift in the doctrine of evil:

Scripture moves from addressing disobedience to addressing incompatibility with life.

The Deluge is not a disciplinary act aimed at reforming humanity. It is a purifying intervention necessitated by the spread of hybrid corruption that has overtaken all flesh. The preservation of Nôach confirms that judgment is selective, intentional, and restorative in purpose—not indiscriminate destruction.

This week provides the framework required to understand later judgments, including fire, exile, and final eradication, without attributing injustice or volatility to Yahuah.

## Alignment Focus — Chapter 3 (The Origin of Evil)

From Chapter 3, students must retain the following interpretive anchors:

- Corruption can affect flesh and creation, not only behavior
- The Nephilim function as agents of systemic violence
- Humanity's destruction is not attributed to original human creation
- Preservation operates through lineage continuity

Judgment functions as purification when restoration is no longer possible

**Key Terms and Definitions (Week 19)**

- Corruption

A condition in which flesh, lineage, and created order are altered beyond restoration through sustained rebellion.

- Violence

The outward manifestation of corruption consuming humanity and creation.

- **Purification**

The removal of corrupted elements to preserve what remains viable within creation.

- **Deluge**

A judicial act of cleansing and containment, not corrective discipline.

# COVENANTAL STUDY TASK

*Engage Chapter 3 directly. Do not import later Yada Yahuah.*

- *Identify how Scripture distinguishes corruption from moral failure*
- *Trace the progression from hybrid activity to total collapse*
- *Explain why forgiveness alone could not address the condition described*
- *Articulate why preservation required removal*

## FINAL THOUGHTS — WEEK 19

"When corruption becomes total, preservation requires removal."

## QUOTE REFLECTION

"Judgment preserves creation when mercy can no longer heal it."

# BODILESS SPIRITS, AGENCY, AND MISATTRIBUTED EVIL
Demons, Maśṭêmâh, and the Restoration of Scriptural Categories

## WEEK 20 LEARNING OUTCOMES — EVIL AGENCY AND SCRIPTURAL PRECISION

By the end of Week 20, students should be able to identify the true agents of evil described in Scripture, distinguishing clearly between angels, demons, and humanity according to origin, assignment, and limitation. Students should demonstrate why demons are not fallen angels, why they emerge only after the Deluge, and why their activity is confined to the earth. Students should also explain the authorized role of Maśṭêmâh and articulate how linguistic confusion leads to false attribution of evil to Yahuah. Finally, students should apply disciplined covenant language to preserve accurate responsibility, judgment, and Yada Yahuah coherence.

## PURPOSE OF WEEK 20

Week 20 restores clarity of agency, which is essential for truthful Yada Yahuah. Chapter 4 resolves a confusion that has corrupted nearly all later doctrine: the failure to distinguish who does evil, who executes judgment, and who authorizes testing. When these categories collapse, evil is either attributed to Yahuah Himself or projected onto an imagined rival deity.

This week trains students to read Scripture with categorical discipline. Demons are not primordial beings, not fallen angels, and not metaphors. Maśṭêmâh is not a rival god, nor the author of creation, but an authorized agent operating within strict limits. Evil is therefore neither divine nor autonomous. It is historical, derivative, and restrained.

## TERM II - MONTH 1- WEEK 20 - READING

Read Chapter 4 from *The Origin of Evil: Biblical Truths Hidden in Plain Sight Origin of Evil Spirits*

- **Chănôk (Enoch) 15:8–12**
  Chapter 4 establishes that demons originate after the extermination of the
  Nephilim. They are the bodiless spirits of hybrid beings who were never part
  of original creation and therefore possess no inheritance, no rest, and no
  place beyond the earth.

  This origin explains their behavior. They afflict, oppress, deceive, and destroy—
  not because they are sovereign, but because they are displaced. Their hostility
  toward humanity arises from origin, not rivalry. They torment humans because
  they proceed from humans.

  This distinction is foundational: **demons are historical consequences of
  rebellion,** not eternal beings created by Yahuah.

### Absence of Demons Before the Deluge
Chapter 4 confirms that prior to the destruction of the Nephilim:
- There were no demons
- There was no systemic disease
- There was no pervasive spiritual affliction

Evil existed as disobedience and violence, but not as an external spiritual
infestation. Demonic activity enters history only after the hybrid race is
destroyed. This chronology eliminates the idea of primordial evil spirits and
preserves the integrity of creation as originally ordered.

### Forbidden Knowledge and the Continuation of Corruption
- **Chănôk 10; 16; 19; 65**
  Human destruction does not persist because of ignorance, but because
  forbidden instruction continues.

Chapter 4 shows that the teachings of the Watchers—and later the influence of demons—drive idolatry, sacrifice, and deception.

Perdition is therefore not accidental. It is sustained through engagement with knowledge that was never authorized for humanity. Scripture consistently links corruption to revelation received unlawfully, not to lack of enlightenment.

## Maśṭêmâh as an Authorized Agent

- **Jubilees 10–11; Hosea 9**

  Maśṭêmâh is not presented as a fallen angel nor as an independent adversary. He is an authorized figure operating under permission. His role is administrative: overseeing permitted testing, accusation, and exposure of human inclination.

Chapter 4 shows that Maśṭêmâh retains access to Yahuah and operates within limits explicitly set by Him. This explains Scriptural testing without introducing a competing or co-eternal power structure.

## Correcting the Fiction of a Rival Deity

Chapter 4 dismantles the later Yada Yahuah invention of a sovereign evil opponent. Scripture presents:

- Bound Watchers
- Wandering spirits with no inheritance
- Authorized testers
- Restricted agents

When all opposition is flattened into a single mythical figure, agency is obscured and responsibility is misplaced. Week 20 restores the Scriptural map.

## Teaching Explanation

Chapter 4 demonstrates that evil is **real, historical, and limited.**

Demons act, deceive, and afflict—but they do not rule. Maśṭêmâh tests—but does not create, corrupt, or reign. Yahuah judges—but does not originate evil. The failure to maintain these distinctions results in Yada Yahuah collapse.

Precision is therefore not academic excess; it is obedience to what Scripture actually reveals.

## ALIGNMENT FOCUS — CHAPTER 4 (THE ORIGIN OF EVIL)

From Chapter 4, students must retain:

- Demons are bodiless spirits of the Nephilim
- Demons originate after the Deluge
- Demons are not angels and not created by Yahuah
- Forbidden knowledge sustains corruption
- Maśṭêmâh operates by permission and limit
- Linguistic confusion causes false attribution of evil

# *COVENANTAL STUDY TASK*

*Engage only Chapter 4 and the cited Scriptures.*

- *Identify the origin, nature, and limitation of demons*
- *Explain why demons cannot be attributed to Yahuah's creative will*
- *Distinguish Maśṭêmâh's role from rebellion*
- *Rewrite one commonly misread passage using disciplined covenant language*

## KEY TERMS AND DEFINITIONS (WEEK 20)

- **Evil Spirits (Demons)**
  Bodiless spirits of the Nephilim, confined to the earth without inheritance or rest.
- **Maśṭêmâh**
  An authorized angelic agent overseeing permitted testing and accusation under divine limit.

- **Agency**
  The responsible actor behind an action or outcome.
- **Covenant Language**
  Scripturally governed vocabulary that preserves correct attribution and responsibility.

## FINAL THOUGHTS ON WEEK 20

When agency is restored, accusation collapses.

## QUOTE REFLECTION

"Confusion survives where language is careless."

# TERM II · MONTH 1 — CONSOLIDATION AND REINFORCEMENT (WEEKS 17-20)
## PURPOSE

This section consolidates the structural foundations of Term II · Month 1. These weeks establish the necessary categories for understanding rebellion, corruption, judgment, and agency before advancing into heavenly administration in Month 2.

If any principle below is unclear, the student must return to the corresponding week before proceeding. Month 2 assumes mastery of these foundations and does not repeat them.

## CORE FOUNDATIONS BY WEEK

Order Precedes Corruption (Week 17)

- All spirits are created within divine order and assignment
- Angels and humans differ by function, not value
- Evil is not a created substance or primordial force
- Deception introduces disobedience without altering the goodness of creation
- Knowledge of evil is acquired through transgression, not divine design

**Key Outcome:**

The student understands that corruption is historical, not intrinsic to creation.

**Rebellion Is Boundary Violation (Week 18)**

- The Watchers were authorized emissaries with a defined mandate
- A single prohibition governed their assignment: no procreation
- Corruption begins through persuasion, oath, and willful defiance
- The covenant of Mount Hermon represents deliberate, irreversible rebellion

Hybridization constitutes a breach of created boundaries established by Yahuah, not a symbolic failure.

**Key Outcome:**

The student can trace corruption to conscious rebellion, not ignorance or emotion.

## Corruption Becomes a Total Condition (Week 19)

Sin as an act differs from corruption as a condition

- The Nephilim are the primary agents of systemic violence
- Corruption spreads into humanity, animals, and the earth itself
- The Deluge responds to total corruption, not ordinary human weakness
- Judgment functions as purification when restoration is no longer possible

**Key Outcome:**

The student understands why judgment escalates only when corruption becomes irreversible.

## Evil Has Personal Agency and Misattributed Origins (Week 20)

- Demons are the bodiless spirits of the Nephilim, not fallen angels
- Evil spirits originate after the Deluge, not at creation
- Forbidden knowledge sustains post-Deluge corruption
- Maśṭêmâh functions as an authorized testing and judgmental agent
- Linguistic confusion falsely attributes evil to Yahuah

**Key Outcome:**

The student can correctly assign agency, responsibility, and action using covenant language.

## Cumulative Month 1 Master Principle

Evil originates through rebellion, boundary violation, and resulting corruption—not in Yahuah's nature, will, or creative design.

Judgment responds to corruption as containment and purification.

Language precision preserves correct attribution of agency and righteousness.

**Mandatory Student Action (Before Proceeding to Month 2)**

- Re-read any week where sequence, agency, or causation remains unclear
- Ensure that creation, rebellion, corruption, and judgment are not collapsed into a single category
- Verify that moral evil, judgment, calamity, and agency are never conflated
- Preserve structural reasoning rather than doctrinal assertion

Failure to master these distinctions will result in misreading heavenly administration in Month 2.

## TERM II · MONTH 2

### Academic Orientation — Term II · Month 2

Month 2 advances Bachelor-level study from definition and covenant language discipline (Month 1) into heavenly administration, celestial accountability, and rebellion in the heavenly realm. Students are expected to preserve Scriptural categories while tracing how corruption spreads through boundary violation, unlawful authority, and forbidden transmission of knowledge.

### This module assumes mastery of Term II · Month 1, especially:

- Evil is not created by Yahuah
- Judgment is not moral evil
- Corruption originates through rebellion
- Covenant language discipline prevents false accusations against Yahuah

### Students are expected to:

- Demonstrate heavenly order and accountability using Scripture
- Dentify rebellion as deliberate boundary violation, not metaphor
- Distinguish authorized knowledge from unlawful transmission by fruit and covenant order
- Explain how judgment functions as containment to preserve creation

Assertions must be supported by the assigned readings and governed by Scriptural reasoning rather than philosophical speculation.

## MODULE OVERVIEW

Rebellion in the Heavenly Realm

**(The Origin of Evil: Biblical Truths Hidden in Plain Sight** — Chapters 5)

This module continues Term II by examining heavenly rebellion beyond humanity, focusing on the Watchers and the violation of heavenly order. Month 2 builds directly on Month 1 by showing that evil does not originate in creation itself, but spreads through boundary violation, unlawful authority, and forbidden transmission of knowledge.

Students will examine how celestial beings were assigned order, authority, and limits—and how rebellion occurred when those limits were rejected. This month exposes the spiritual dimension of corruption and explains why evil cannot be reduced to metaphor, formation, or symbolism alone.

**By the end of this month, the student will understand that:**
- The heavenly realm operates under order and accountability
- Celestial beings are not autonomous or morally neutral
- The Watchers violated assigned boundaries
- Forbidden knowledge was transmitted unlawfully
- Heavenly rebellion produced lasting earthly consequences

This month prepares the student for deeper study of corruption, violence, hybridization, judgment, and restoration in later terms.

**Methodological Continuity — Heavenly Order, Boundary, and Agency**

This module continues the Scripture-first methodology established in Term II · Month 1. All material in Month 2 is governed by the following principles:
- **Scripture Establishes Order Before Describing Rebellion**
  Heavenly rebellion is intelligible only if heavenly order, assignment, and limits are first established from Scripture.
- **Celestial Beings Are Accountable Under Authority**
  Celestial beings are not autonomous or morally neutral; they operate within assigned roles and boundaries.
- **Rebellion Is Willful Boundary Violation**
  Curiosity and desire are distinguished from rebellion by intent, oath, and defiance of assigned limits.
- **Forbidden Knowledge Corrupts Because It Bypasses Covenant Order**
  Knowledge must be evaluated by authorization and fruit; unlawful transmission produces deception and long-term corruption.
- **Judgment Responds to Corruption and Contains It**
  Judgment is interpreted as measured containment of destruction, not moral

evil originating in Yahuah.

These principles govern all readings, study tasks, and assessments in Term II · Month 2.

**Module Learning Outcomes — Term II · Month 2**

**By the end of Term II · Month 2, students should be able to:**
- Demonstrate that the heavenly realm operates under order, assignment, and accountability
- Identify the Watchers as historical celestial beings and define their transgression as boundary violation
- Distinguish curiosity, desire, and affection from rebellion rooted in intent and oath
- Explain how forbidden knowledge functions as a mechanism of corruption
- Trace continuity patterns of rebellion from Eden through later historical manifestations
- Explain why judgment functions as containment rather than moral evil, preserving Yahuah's character

Mastery is demonstrated through accurate citation of assigned texts, coherent covenantal reasoning, and disciplined preservation of Scriptural categories.

## CHAPTER COVERAGE
**The Origin of Evil — Chapters 5–8**
- **Chapter 5 — Heavenly Administration and Adversarial Testing**
  (Maśṭêmâh, delegated authority, testing, accusation, and lawful judgment)
- **Chapter 6 — The Power of Demons**
  (How unclean spirits dominate through fear and ignorance)
- **Chapter 7 — The Two Seeds**
  (The pure line of Yahuah and the corrupted lineage of the Nephilim)
- **Chapter 8 — Sodom and Gomorrah**
  (Cities that symbolize the fullness of sin and the justice of Yahuah)

# HEAVENLY ADMINISTRATION AND ACCUSATION

Delegated Testing, Judgment, and the Adversary's Role

## WEEK 21 LEARNING OUTCOMES — HEAVENLY ADMINISTRATION & TESTING

By the end of Week 21, students should be able to:

- Explain how heavenly testing operates without originating moral evil
- dentify Maśṭêmâh as an adversarial agent operating under divine authority, not as a rival power
- Distinguish delegated judgment from divine authorship of destruction
- Demonstrate how accusation, testing, restraint, and release function within heavenly order
- Preserve the righteousness of Yahuah while accounting for testing, calamity, and judgment

## PURPOSE OF WEEK 21

Week 21 establishes the administrative mechanics of the heavenly court as revealed in Scripture.

Before rebellion, corruption, or destruction are examined further, Scripture clarifies how testing and accusation function within divine order.

Chapter 5 corrects a deeply embedded Yada Yahuah error: the assumption that Yahuah personally performs acts of cruelty, temptation, or destruction. Instead, Scripture reveals delegated testing and delegated execution, governed by permission, restraint, and timing.

This week equips students to read difficult passages without collapsing agency upward. Without this framework, later judgment narratives are misread as divine volatility rather than judicial consistency.

Read Chapter 5 from *The Origin of Evil: Biblical Truths Hidden in Plain Sight*
*(Faith against accusation — The heavenly dialogue that unleashed the test of sacrifice)*

The readings below are not included to retell Chapter 5, but to train students to identify agency, permission, and execution.

## The Test of Abraham: Accusation Behind the Command

- Berēšhīṯh (Genesis) 22:1–2, 9–12
- Yôbêl (Jubilees) 17:16; 18:9–11

Genesis records the test; Jubilees reveals its heavenly origin.

The challenge to sacrifice Yitschâq does not originate from divine desire for violence, but from Maśṭêmâh's accusation against Abraham's faith.

## Students must observe the juridical sequence:

- Accusation is raised
- Permission is granted
- Testing is executed
- Obedience silences accusation
- Restraint halts destruction

The test does not reveal cruelty in Yahuah — it exposes fidelity in Abraham and shames the accuser.

## Abraham's Blessing and Knowledge of the Adversary

- Yôbêl (Jubilees) 19:28

Abraham's blessing over Yaʿaqôb explicitly names Maśṭêmâh and invokes protection from his spirits. This demonstrates that the patriarchs possessed clear knowledge of heavenly administration, later obscured by tradition.

Students must note that covenant blessing includes recognition of adversarial presence, not denial of it.

### The Attempted Death of Môsheh Explained
- Šhemōṯ (Exodus) 4:24–26
- Yôbêl (Jubilees) 48:2–4

Exodus alone appears to implicate Yahuah as aggressor. Jubilees restores agency, revealing Maśṭêmâh as the attacker, acting to prevent the deliverance of Yâshâral.

### This passage trains students in a critical discipline:
Scripture must be interpreted with clarified agency, not assumed causation. Yahuah rescues Môsheh; He does not sabotage His own mission.

### Maśṭêmâh Behind the Oppression of Egypt
- Yôbêl (Jubilees) 48:9–13

Maśṭêmâh is shown operating behind Mitsrayim, empowering resistance and sorcery. Yahuah permits opposition, restrains remedies, and ultimately overrules through judgment.
The hardening of Pharaoh's heart is not divine malice but the exposure of pride under permitted resistance.

### Binding of the Accuser During Redemption
- Yôbêl (Jubilees) 48:15–18

Maśṭêmâh is temporarily bound so that he cannot accuse Yâshâral during deliverance. Accusation is therefore neither constant nor absolute; it is restrained according to covenant purpose.
Judgment includes not only punishment of enemies, but restriction of the accuser.

### The Death of the Firstborn: Execution Clarified
- Šhemōṯ (Exodus) 12:23, 29
- Yôbêl (Jubilees) 49:2

Scripture distinguishes between Yahuah passing over and the destroyer executing death. Jubilees identifies the destroyer as Maśṭêmâh and his agents. This distinction is non-negotiable:

Yahuah authorizes judgment; He does not personally destroy.

## "Satan" as Title, Not Name

- Îyôb (Job) 1:6–7

The term *śâṭân* functions as a role — adversary, accuser — not as a proper name or rival deity. *Maśṭêmâh* fulfills this role within heavenly order.

Students must learn to resist later Yada Yahuah inventions that flatten Scriptural categories into a single mythical enemy.

## Teaching Explanation

Week 21 reveals that opposition exists within order.

Maśṭêmâh is not a rebel Watcher, not a sovereign enemy, and not a corrupt originator of evil. He is an authorized adversary, permitted to test, accuse, and execute judgment within strict limits.

Yahuah remains righteous, restrained, and sovereign.

Testing refines faith; accusation exposes loyalty; judgment preserves order.

This framework prevents Yada Yahuah collapse by preserving correct agency.

## Alignment Focus — Chapter 5 *(The Origin of Evil)*

From Chapter 5, students must retain:

- Testing does not equal moral evil
- Maśṭêmâh operates by permission, not autonomy
- Accusation precedes testing
- Judgment is executed through agents
- Restraint governs destruction
- Yahuah never acts as destroyer or tempter

## KEY TERMS AND DEFINITIONS (WEEK 21)

- Adversary (śâṭân): A functional role of accusation or opposition, not a proper name

- Maśṭêmâh: An authorized angelic agent tasked with testing, accusation, and execution under limit
- Delegated Judgment: Judgment carried out by authorized agents rather than by Yahuah directly
- Testing: A permitted process that reveals faithfulness without originating evil

# COVENANTAL STUDY TASK
*Using Chapter 5 only:*
- **Explain why Abraham's test does not implicate Yahuah in cruelty**
- **Distinguish divine permission from divine action**
- **Trace Maśṭêmâh's role across Abraham, Môsheh, and Egypt**
- **Demonstrate how this framework preserves Yahuah's righteousness**

## FINAL THOUGHTS — WEEK 21

"Judgment does not require corruption; testing does not require cruelty."

Without this week, later doctrine collapses into accusation against Yahuah.

With it, rebellion, corruption, and judgment remain intelligible, measured, and just.

## QUOTE REFLECTION

"When accusation is understood, righteousness no longer needs defense."

## TERM II · MONTH 2 — WEEK 22
# THE POWER AND LIMITS OF DEMONIC INFLUENCE
How Rebellion Persists Without Authority

## LEARNING OUTCOMES

By the end of this week, the student will be able to:

- Distinguish influence from authority within post-judgment rebellion
- Identify how rebellion persists without lawful power or command
- Maintain correct attribution of agency and accountability in the presence of deception
- Interpret post-Flood corruption without inflating demonic capacity
- Preserve the sovereignty of Yahuah while explaining the continued presence of evil

## PURPOSE OF WEEK 22

Week 21 established that heavenly order operates through delegation, jurisdiction, and accountability, even in matters of testing and accusation.
Week 22 addresses the juridical question that necessarily follows:
If transgressive beings were judged and confined, by what mechanism does corruption continue within history?
The purpose of this week is to discipline the student against a foundational interpretive error: the assumption that ongoing activity implies ongoing authority. Chapter 6 must be read not as an expansion of evil's power, but as a clarification of its limits.

## TERM II – MONTH 2 – WEEK 22 - READING

Read Chapter 6 from *The Origin of Evil* with deliberate attention to constraint, not spectacle.

**The student must resist reading for:**

- sensational claims,
- mythological amplification, or

- explanations that shift responsibility away from covenant agents.

**Instead, read for:**
- what capacities are explicitly denied,
- what boundaries are preserved after judgment, and
- how Scripture maintains order even in corruption.
- Chapter 6 functions as a corrective lens, not an imaginative narrative.

## Teaching Explanation

This chapter requires disciplined reading because it dismantles the assumption that evil persists because it possesses strength, rank, or jurisdiction.

As the student reads, observe how activity is described without conferring authority. The text consistently reframes demonic operation as dependent, parasitic, and restricted, rather than autonomous or commanding.

## The instructional task is to recognize how Scripture allows for:
- persistence without permission,
- influence without command, and
- deception without coercion,

all while preserving human agency and divine sovereignty.

## Alignment Focus chapter 6 (The Origin of Evil)

The student must maintain strict category separation throughout Chapter 6:
- Authority belongs only to covenant alignment
- Influence operates where discernment is absent
- Judgment restrains scope, not memory or inheritance
- Transmission occurs through lineage and continuity, not command

Chapter 6 does not introduce new powers or rival sovereignties. It clarifies how previously judged corruption continues to echo within creation without violating established order.

# KEY TERMS WEEK 22

- **Authority vs. Influence** – *Authority* is delegated right to command and govern within assigned bounds, while *influence* is the ability to persuade without lawful mandate or jurisdiction.
- **Jurisdiction** – The defined sphere or boundary within which authority is legitimately exercised and outside of which action becomes transgressive.
- **Covenant Alignment** – The state of being ordered rightly under Yahuah's commands, purposes, and assigned roles within the covenant structure.
- **Inheritance** – That which is lawfully received by assignment or promise, rather than seized by desire or force.
- **Restraint** – The intentional limitation of action in obedience to Yahuah's given boundaries and prohibitions.
- **Accountability** – The obligation to answer for actions taken within or beyond one's assigned authority.
- **Containment** – The maintenance of order through enforced boundaries that prevent the spread or escalation of corruption.

# COVENANTAL STUDY TASK

*As you study Chapter 6, identify every place where limits are emphasized rather than actions.*

*For each section, ask:*

*• What cannot occur because judgment has already been rendered?*

*• Where does responsibility remain human rather than external?*

*• How does covenant obedience function as a boundary condition?*

Record observations analytically. Do not summarize or retell the chapter.

## FINAL THOUGHTS

Week 22 disciplines the student against exaggeration. Evil is not elevated, dramatized, or granted sovereignty it does not possess. Continued corruption does not testify to rival power, but to unresolved transmission under restraint.

Correct reading preserves Yahuah's sovereignty, safeguards human accountability, and prevents Yada Yahuah distortion.

## QUOTE REFLECTION

"Fear magnifies what ignorance misunderstands."

Reflect on how misunderstanding limits produces misplaced fear—and how covenant discernment restores order.

# FORBIDDEN KNOWLEDGE AND THE TWO SEEDS
Discernment Under Conditions of Mixture

## LEARNING OUTCOMES
By the end of this week, the student will be able to:
- Apply covenantal reasoning to conditions of **mixture after judgment**
- Distinguish between origin of corruption and **transmission** of corruption
- Evaluate knowledge claims by **authorization and fruit**, not antiquity or concealment
- Read lineage and identity **without relying on appearance or geography**
- Preserve assigned authority by resisting premature judgment or separation

## PURPOSE OF WEEK 23
**Weeks 21–22 established two critical controls:**
heavenly administration operates lawfully, and post-judgment rebellion persists without authority.

Week 23 advances the inquiry by addressing a deeper structural problem:
*How does corruption reproduce itself—intellectually, generationally, and covenantally—once judgment has already occurred?*

The purpose of this week is to train the student to read Chapter 7 **as a methodological chapter,** not a genealogical curiosity. Once mixture exists, discernment must replace visibility, and covenant criteria must replace surface evaluation.

## TERM II - MONTH 2 - WEEK 23 - READING
Read Chapter 7 from The Origin of Evil with attention to classification and criteria, not narrative expansion.

**The student must read for:**

- how Scripture defines conditions, not merely recounts events,
- how evaluation shifts from separation by location to discernment by fruit, and
- how judgment timing governs human restraint.

Chapter 7 requires disciplined reading because it establishes rules for interpretation under mixed historical conditions.

## Teaching Explanation

This chapter must be read as a correction to the assumption that judgment restores simplicity.

The student is trained to recognize that post-Flood history operates under **overlapping conditions,** where corruption and covenant fidelity coexist within the same visible field. As a result, identity can no longer be inferred reliably from lineage claims, external affiliation, or proximity to covenant communities.

Observe how the chapter consistently shifts responsibility toward **discernment governed by outcome,** while restricting human authority to evaluate, expose, or separate prematurely.

## Alignment Focus Chapter 7 (The Origin of Evil)

The student must preserve the following analytical boundaries while reading Chapter 7:

- Corruption **originates** in transgression but **persists** through transmission
- Knowledge is judged by **authorization and obedience**, not preservation or age
- Mixture introduces **coexistence,** not approval
- Final separation is **assigned,** not delegated to human agents

Chapter 7 does not authorize speculation or zeal-driven identification. It enforces covenant discipline under conditions where boundaries are no longer externally visible.

## KEY TERMS WEEK 23

- **Two Conditions** – The distinction between obedience and transgression, under which all covenant actions and outcomes are evaluated.
- **Transmission** – The passing of influence, knowledge, or corruption from one party to another through instruction, imitation, or participation.
- **Forbidden Knowledge** – Information or practices withheld by Yahuah because their possession or use violates assigned boundaries and results in corruption rather than wisdom.
- **Mixture** – The unlawful blending of what Yahuah has ordered to remain distinct, resulting in distortion of purpose and nature.
- **Covenant Authorization** – The explicit divine permission that legitimizes action within a defined role, office, or assignment.
- **Discernment by Fruit** – The evaluation of legitimacy and alignment based on observable outcomes rather than claimed authority or intention.
- **Assigned Judgment** – The specific form of consequence determined by Yahuah and applied according to the nature of the transgression and the role of the transgressor.

# COVENANTAL STUDY TASK

*Produce a short analytic reading (not devotional reflection)*
*addressing the following:*

- **Explain how forbidden knowledge can re-enter history without renewed angelic descent, using Chapter 7's logic.**
- **Identify how the Qeynan account functions as a warning about transmission, not innovation.**
- **Define discernment by fruit as a methodological rule for mixed conditions, using Matthew 13 as the governing frame.**
- **Explain why premature human separation violates assigned authority and covenant order.**

Maintain controlled language and covenant categories throughout.

## FINAL THOUGHTS

Week 23 disciplines the student against superficial certainty. Once mixture becomes historical reality, visibility ceases to be reliable. Knowledge, identity, and allegiance must be evaluated by outcome, authorization, and obedience—not by claims, proximity, or antiquity. Discernment is no longer optional; it is the required covenant response to a mixed world.

## QUOTE REFLECTION

"Knowledge without obedience becomes a weapon."

Reflect on how detachment from covenant order transforms preservation into corruption.

## TERM II · MONTH 2 — WEEK 24
# CONSEQUENCES
Judgment, Containment, and Historical Manifestation

## LEARNING OUTCOMES

By the end of this week, the student will be able to:

- Explain why divine judgment follows fullness of corruption as containment rather than cruelty
- Distinguish moral reductionism from covenantal categories such as boundary, lineage, and irreversibility
- Identify how Watcher-level corruption re-manifests historically after prior judgments
- Trace how rebellion persists through knowledge transmission and household patterns
- Preserve Yahuah's righteousness by separating cause (rebellion) from response (judgment)

## PURPOSE OF WEEK 24

Weeks 21–23 established lawful heavenly order, post-judgment persistence without authority, and the mixed condition of humanity after Babel.
Week 24 completes Month 2 by training the student to read outcomes, not merely actions.

The central question addressed is not whether judgment occurs, but why it occurs when it does:

When corruption returns after prior judgment, how does Scripture show Yahuah responding—and on what covenantal basis?
The purpose of this week is to prevent the student from interpreting judgment as instability, excess, or moral reaction. Chapter 8 requires disciplined reading

that understands judgment as containment of a threat to creation.

## TERM II – MONTH 2 – WEEK 24 – READING

Read Chapter 8 from The Origin of Evil with attention to thresholds and outcomes, not isolated behaviors.

**The student must resist readings that:**
- reduce judgment to single acts or modern moral categories, or
- portray divine response as impulsive or emotionally driven.

**Instead, read for:**
- how Scripture identifies fullness as a condition,
- how investigation precedes decree, and
- how judgment functions to limit further spread.

Chapter 8 must be read as a case study in consequence, not as a morality tale.

**Teaching Explanation**

This chapter trains the student to recognize that judgment in Scripture is often triggered not by isolated transgression, but by systemic concentration of corruption.

**Observe how the narrative structure emphasizes:**
- assessment before action,
- covenant disclosure rather than secrecy, and
- removal of a population as a means of preserving creation.

The student must also note that judgment does not erase memory, habit, or learned disorder. Chapter 8 therefore requires attention to aftermath, showing how corrupted patterns can persist even after physical deliverance.

**Alignment Focus of Chapter 8 (The Origin of Evil)**

While reading Chapter 8, the student must preserve the following Month 2 controls:

- Judgment responds to irreversibility, not mere prevalence
- Containment protects creation; it does not originate evil
- Boundary violation targets created order, not only ethics
- Consequence can extend through household and lineage, not only location
- Watcher corruption persists primarily through transmitted mysteries, not renewed descent

Chapter 8 does not contradict earlier judgments; it demonstrates how corruption re-concentrates and how Scripture responds consistently.

## KEY TERMS WEEK 24
- Fullness (of corruption): a threshold where corruption becomes concentrated, normalized, and self-sustaining
- Containment: divine limitation or removal designed to preserve creation
- Boundary Violation: targeting prohibited realms, unions, or acts that corrupt order
- Decretive Judgment: judgment established against an enduring corrupt outcome
- Watcher Legacy: corruption transmitted through hidden teachings and mysteries

# COVENANTAL STUDY TASK

*Pause your reading and complete the following using covenantal categories only:*

- *From Genesis 18–19 and Jubilees 16, identify indicators of fullness rather than isolated sin.*
- *Explain why the destruction functions as containment of corruption, not moral evil in Yahuah.*
- *Using Enoch 10:7 and 16:3, explain how transmitted teachings operate as an enduring mechanism of corruption after major judgments.*

Do not summarize narrative events. Analyze conditions and responses.

## FINAL THOUGHTS

Week 24 requires the student to read judgment with covenant precision. Sodom and Gomorrah are presented as an outcome, not an anomaly. When corruption reorganizes itself as collective defiance and no remnant remains, judgment functions as restraint.

The student is not permitted to interpret this as divine cruelty or instability. It is presented as preservation of creation when covenant order can no longer rehabilitate what has become irreversible.

## QUOTE REFLECTION

"Judgment restrains what covenant order cannot rehabilitate."

Reflect on how restraint preserves creation when restoration is no longer possible.

# TERM II· MONTH 2 — REINFORCEMENT TO DO (WEEKS 21–24)

## PURPOSE

This section reinforces the core foundations of Month 2. If any principle below is unclear, the student must return to the corresponding week before proceeding.

### Heavenly Order Is Assigned and Accountable (Week 21)

- Heavenly beings operate under delegated authority, assignment, and limits
- Accountability presupposes jurisdiction, restraint, and measurable transgression

### Rebellion Is Boundary Violation (Week 22)

- The Watchers transgressed knowingly and deliberately
- Intent, oath, and foreknowledge distinguish rebellion from ignorance, metaphor, or symbolism

### Forbidden Knowledge Spreads Corruption (Week 23)

- Knowledge must be evaluated by authorization and fruit, not antiquity or sophistication
- Unlawful transmission accelerates deception, disorder, and long-term corruption

### Judgment Functions as Containment (Week 24)

- Judgment follows the fullness of corruption, not isolated failure
- Containment preserves creation and restrains further spread of destruction

### Cumulative Month 2 Master Principle

Heavenly rebellion violates assigned order; unlawful knowledge spreads corruption; judgment restrains corruption in order to preserve creation.

### Mandatory Student Action (Before Month 3)

- Re-read any week where confusion remains

- Preserve Scriptural categories: order, rebellion, knowledge, containment
- Do not collapse judgment into moral evil or attribute corruption to Yahuah

**Assessment Alignment — Term II · Month 2**
- Week 21 establishes heavenly order, assignment, and accountability
- Week 22 defines rebellion as boundary violation and authority abuse
- Week 23 explains how corruption spreads through unlawful transmission of knowledge
- Week 24 demonstrates judgment as containment through historical manifestation and consequence

Students must integrate all four dimensions—order, rebellion, transmission, and containment—into one coherent Scriptural explanation that preserves the character of Yahuah.

# MONTH 2 ESSAY — TERM II – MONTH 2

**Bachelor-Level Assessment**

**Length:** 2,000–2,500 words

**Prompt**

Explain how heavenly order and assigned boundaries establish accountability in the celestial realm. Define the Watchers' sin as Scriptural rebellion rather than symbolism, and demonstrate how unlawful transmission of knowledge accelerates corruption throughout human history. Conclude by explaining how judgment functions as containment rather than moral evil, thereby preserving the character of Yahuah.

**Evaluation Criteria**
- Scriptural category precision (order, rebellion, corruption, judgment)
- Logical progression supported by assigned texts
- Covenantal Reasoning with disciplined use of Scriptural and Second Temple witnesses
- Absence of philosophical speculation
- Preservation of Yahuah's moral purity and covenant integrity

## TERM II · MONTH 3
# ACADEMIC ORIENTATION — TERM II · MONTH 3

Month 3 advances Bachelor-level study from heavenly rebellion (Month 2) into the created-order consequences of that rebellion. The focus shifts from authority and judgment in the heavenly realm to boundary violation within creation itself—specifically kinds, hybridization, Nephilim lineage, and the Flood as an act of preservation.

Students must preserve Scriptural categories of kinds, boundaries, corruption, and containment while tracing how rebellion moves from heaven into flesh, persists through lineage and history, and reemerges after judgment under altered conditions.

## THIS MODULE ASSUMES MASTERY OF TERM II · MONTHS 1-2, ESPECIALLY:

- Yahuah is not the source of moral or structural evil
- Judgment functions as containment and preservation, not cruelty
- Rebellion is measurable because order and boundaries are real
- Unlawful transmission (whether authority, seed, or knowledge) accelerates corruption

**Students are expected to:**

- Demonstrate that "kinds" and separation are creation principles established by Yahuah
- Identify hybridization as boundary violation expressed in flesh, not symbolism or metaphor
- Establish Nephilim identity as a historical doctrinal category using assigned Scriptural witnesses
- Explain the Flood as preservation of creation from irreversible corruption
- Trace how corruption reemerges after the Flood through spirits, deception, and preserved systems rather than renewed hybridization

All assertions must be governed by the assigned readings and Scriptural reasoning, not philosophical speculation or later Yada Yahuah systems.

## MODULE OVERVIEW
Hybridization, the Nephilim, and Containment Judgment
*(The Origin of Evil — Chapters 9–12)*

This module continues the progression of The Origin of Evil by examining hybridization as the primary mechanism through which corruption entered the created order. Month 3 builds directly on the study of the Watchers by demonstrating the **biological, covenantal, and historical consequences** of boundary violation.

Students will learn why the Nephilim are not symbolic figures or literary exaggerations, but a **real doctrinal category** resulting from unlawful mixing. This corruption reached a level that required global judgment—not to punish humanity emotionally, but to preserve creation structurally.

This month also explains why corruption did not end with the Flood and why, after containment, rebellion reappears in altered form—through spirits, doctrines, systems, and opposition to Yahuah's covenant.

**By the end of this month, the student will understand that:**
- Creation was established with fixed kinds and boundaries
- Hybridization violates divine order and corrupts flesh
- The Nephilim result from unlawful mixing, not myth
- The Flood was a necessary act of containment and preservation
- Corruption reemerges post-Flood through surviving Nephilim lineage and renewed mixture with humanity.

This month establishes the framework needed to interpret later Scriptural material involving Giants (Nephilim), warfare, conquest narratives, and restoration boundaries without collapsing judgment into cruelty or symbolism.

## Methodological Continuity — Boundaries, Kinds, Corruption, and Containment

This module continues the Scripture-first methodology established in Term II · Months 1–2. All material in Month 3 is governed by the following principles:

- **Creation Order Includes Kinds and Separation**
  "Kinds" and boundaries are treated as divine design embedded in creation, not cultural constructs or metaphors.

- **Hybridization Is Corruption, Not Diversity**
  Mixing that violates divine limits is presented as disorder that spreads into flesh, lineage, and covenant history.

- **Nephilim Are a Doctrinal Category With Historical Continuity**
  The Nephilim are treated as embodied beings produced through unlawful union, with post-Flood continuity demonstrated in Scripture.

- **Judgment Preserves Creation When Corruption Becomes Irreversible**
  The Flood is interpreted as containment and preservation of creation, not emotional reaction or moral overreach.

- **Post-Judgment Corruption Must Be Traced by Agency, Bloodline, and Fruit**
  After the Flood, corruption reemerges through surviving Nephilim bloodline admixture, disembodied spirits, systems, deception, and preserved structures; therefore, students must trace corruption by agency, lineage, and fruit rather than assume eradication through judgment alone.

These principles govern all readings, instructional explanations, study tasks, and assessments in Term II · Month 3.

## CHAPTER COVERAGE
### *The Origin of Evil — Chapters 9–12*

- **Chapter 9 — Teachings of the Watchers** *(The mysteries revealed by the fallen: magic, war, the heavens, and the root of human occultism)*
- **Chapter 10 — Giants (Nephilim)** *in the Days of Dâwid (The final war between the servants of Yahuah and the descendants of the Giants (Nephilim))*
- **Chapter 11 — Remnant of the Nephilim in New Testament Times** *(The infiltration of the accursed lineage in the apostolic era)*
- **Chapter 12 — Demons (Nephilim)** in the New Testament *(Evidence of the fallen lineage operating under the guise of possession and disease)*

## MODULE LEARNING OUTCOMES — TERM II · MONTH 3

By the end of Term II · Month 3, students should be able to:

- Demonstrate from Scripture that creation is established with kinds, separation, and boundaries
- Define hybridization as boundary violation that produces corruption in flesh
- Establish Nephilim identity and post-Flood continuity using assigned readings and canonical testimony
- Explain why the Flood functioned as containment and preservation rather than cruelty
- Trace how corruption reemerges after the Flood through surviving Nephilim bloodline admixture, disembodied spirits, deception, and preserved rebellious systems.
- Distinguish between pre-Flood corruption expressed through hybrid flesh and post-Flood corruption sustained through surviving Nephilim lineage, disembodied spirits, and systemic structures.

Mastery is demonstrated through accurate citation of assigned texts, coherent covenantal reasoning, and disciplined preservation of Scriptural categories.

# HYBRIDIZATION OF KNOWLEDGE

Forbidden Instruction and Boundary Collapse

## *LEARNING OUTCOMES*

By the end of this week, the student will be able to:

- Distinguish divinely authorized knowledge from forbidden instruction
- Explain why Watcher teachings constitute boundary violation, not neutral advancement
- Identify how unlawful knowledge corrupts culture, warfare, medicine, and worship
- Demonstrate that occult systems originate in Watcher transmission, not human discovery
- Trace how instructional hybridization precedes and necessitates judgment

### PURPOSE OF WEEK 25

Month 2 established that rebellion violates assigned authority and that judgment functions as containment. Month 3 now examines how corruption embeds itself within civilization.

Week 25 focuses on instruction rather than beings.
Scripture does not present the Watchers' transgression as physical rebellion alone. Their most enduring violation was instruction without authorization—the transfer of mysteries preserved in heaven into human stewardship.
The purpose of this week is to train the student to recognize that hybridization is not limited to bloodlines. It also occurs when knowledge crosses forbidden boundaries, reshaping culture and allegiance in ways that persist long after the original rebellion.

## TERM II - MONTH 3 - WEEK 25 - READING

Read Chapter 9 from The Origin of Evil with attention to origin and authorization, not usefulness or sophistication.

**The student must resist evaluating practices by:**

- technological benefit,
- antiquity, or
- cultural normalization.

**Instead, read for:**

- where knowledge originates,
- whether it was withheld for protection, and
- how Scripture treats instruction detached from obedience.

Chapter 9 must be approached as a genealogy of corruption, not a catalog of skills.

**Teaching Explanation**

This chapter requires disciplined reading because it reframes progress itself as a covenant question.

As the student reads, observe how Scripture consistently judges knowledge not by outcome alone, but by boundary crossing. Instruction becomes corrupt when it transfers what was preserved in heaven into human hands without authorization.

The chapter establishes a core interpretive rule:
Knowledge severed from obedience does not remain neutral—it reshapes **desire, allegiance, and worship.**

Watcher instruction produces a secondary form of hybridization: the fusion of heavenly mysteries with corrupted intent. The result is not wisdom, but distortion.

**Alignment Focus of Chapter 9 (The Origin of Evil)**

While reading Chapter 9, the student must preserve the following distinctions:

- Not all knowledge is equal; authorization governs legitimacy
- Forbidden instruction constitutes rebellion, not discovery
- Cultural systems can carry inherited corruption
- Utility does not sanctify origin
- Judgment follows instructional collapse, not ignorance

Chapter 9 does not require the student to list practices exhaustively. It trains the student to recognize the fingerprints of unauthorized instruction across Scripture and history.

## KEY TERMS WEEK 25

- Forbidden Knowledge: instruction transmitted outside divine authorization
- Hybridization (Instructional): unlawful fusion of heavenly mysteries with human culture
- Occult Systems: frameworks originating in Watcher transmission, marked by secrecy and control
- Authorization: divine permission that determines whether knowledge preserves or corrupts creation

# COVENANTAL STUDY TASK

*Engage the Scriptural witnesses directly and complete the following analytically:*

- **Identify two Watcher teachings and explain why origin, not usefulness, renders them corrupt.**
- **Explain how forbidden knowledge represents boundary violation rather than neutral skill.**
- **Demonstrate why Scripture treats occult wisdom as rebellion against trust in Yahuah's governance.**

Maintain covenantal categories. Avoid modern moral or technological justifications.

## FINAL THOUGHTS

Week 25 disciplines the student against equating knowledge with progress. Scripture presents corruption not as ignorance, but as unauthorized knowing—truth seized rather than entrusted.

Civilizations do not fall first through immorality, but through instruction that teaches humans to cross boundaries they were never meant to approach.

## QUOTE REFLECTION

"Wisdom submitted preserves life; knowledge seized destroys it."

Reflect on how submission governs whether knowledge heals or corrupts.

## TERM II· MONTH 3 — WEEK 26
# THE NEPHILIM
Identity, Origin, and Historical Continuity

**Learning Outcomes**

By the end of this week, the student will be able to:

- Demonstrate that the Nephilim constitute a continuous Scriptural category, not a pre-Flood anomaly
- Identify Giants (Nephilim) in the historical record as descendants of corrupted lineages
- Explain why conflicts involving Giants (Nephilim) are framed as covenantal necessity, not ethnic aggression
- Distinguish metaphorical readings from genealogical and textual continuity
- Integrate Nephilim presence into the broader framework of hybridization, rebellion, and containment

## PURPOSE OF WEEK 26

Week 26 requires the student to confront a persistent interpretive failure: the assumption that the Nephilim disappear after the Flood.

Having established in Week 25 that corruption embeds itself through unauthorized instruction, Scripture now compels attention to embodied persistence. Chapter 10 demonstrates that rebellion does not remain abstract or ideological. It seeks continuity through flesh, lineage, geography, and power. The purpose of this week is not to sensationalize Giants (Nephilim), but to restore Scriptural coherence by reading later conflicts as the outworking of earlier boundary violations.

## TERM II - MONTH 3 - WEEK 26 - READING

Read Chapter 10 from The Origin of Evil with attention to continuity and classification, not isolated episodes.

**The student must resist:**

- symbolic reductionism,
- mythologizing explanations, or
- readings that sever later texts from earlier genealogical frameworks.

**Instead, read for:**

- how names, locations, and lineages are preserved,
- how conflicts recur in patterned ways, and
- how Scripture consistently treats Giants (Nephilim) as identifiable populations, not literary devices.

Chapter 10 must be read as a historical ledger, not an allegory.

**Teaching Explanation**

This chapter trains the student to recognize that Scripture maintains memory across generations.

**Observe how Giants (Nephilim) appear:**

- tied to specific peoples,
- associated with defined territories, and
- confronted through targeted action rather than generalized judgment.

The student must learn that wars involving Giants (Nephilim) are not framed as expansionist violence or fear of difference. They are presented as acts of containment, consistent with prior judgments against corrupted creation. Chapter 10 therefore reinforces a governing rule of this course:

When corruption survives judgment, judgment reappears in history.

**Alignment Focus with chapter 10 (The Origin of Evil)**

While reading Chapter 10, the student must preserve the following controls:

- Nephilim identity is genealogical, not symbolic
- Giant clans are treated as historical populations
- Warfare against them serves covenantal preservation, not nationalism

- Their eradication aligns with earlier containment judgments
- Physical removal addresses embodied corruption, not ideology alone

Chapter 10 prevents the student from collapsing continuity into metaphor and preserves the integrity of Scriptural testimony.

## KEY TERMS WEEK 26
- Nephilim: hybrid beings originating from unlawful Watcher–human unions
- Giants (Nephilim): embodied descendants of Nephilim bloodlines
- Lineage: transmission of corruption through flesh and genealogy
- Containment: covenantal removal of embodied rebellion

# COVENANTAL STUDY TASK

*Engage the assigned Scriptural witnesses directly. Do not speculate beyond them.*

- ***Explain why Scripture treats Giants (Nephilim) as historical beings rather than symbolic exaggerations.***
- ***Trace Nephilim lineage persistence after the Flood using at least two Scriptural witnesses.***
- ***Explain why the defeat of Giants (Nephilim) under Dâwid is framed as covenantal necessity, not ethnic conflict.***

Maintain juridical and covenantal categories throughout.

## FINAL THOUGHTS

Week 26 disciplines the student against abstraction. Scripture records the defeat of Giants (Nephilim) not to glorify violence, but to testify that corruption which enters flesh must be addressed within history.

Rebellion seeks continuity through bodies and power. Covenant order responds with restraint, judgment, and removal—preserving creation where corruption has taken form.

## QUOTE REFLECTION

"When rebellion takes form, history must respond."

Reflect on how embodied corruption necessitates concrete covenantal response.

# THE FLOOD AND ITS AFTERMATH
Judgment Beyond Forgiveness

## LEARNING OUTCOMES

By the end of this week, the student will be able to:

- Explain why the Flood addressed corruption that forgiveness alone could not heal
- Distinguish judgment as preservation from emotional or retaliatory punishment
- Identify Scriptural indicators of post-Flood remnant corruption
- Demonstrate how Second Temple leadership reflects lineage continuity, not neutral religiosity
- Explain why Yahusha and Yôchânân confront origin and lineage, not merely behavior

## PURPOSE OF WEEK 27

Week 27 reframes the Flood as a measured act of preservation, not a failure of mercy.

Scripture consistently teaches that while moral transgression can be forgiven, corruption that alters created order, flesh, and authority structures cannot simply be absolved. Chapter 11 therefore addresses the necessary Yada Yahuah question:

If the Flood destroyed corrupted flesh, why does Scripture still confront demonic lineage and rebellion in the New Testament era?

The purpose of this week is to train the student to recognize that the Flood functioned as containment, not final eradication. Judgment restrained corruption until the appointed time when confrontation, exposure, and separation could occur within history.

## TERM II – MONTH 3 – WEEK 27 – READING

Read Chapter 11 with attention to continuity rather than rupture.

**The student must resist readings that:**

- isolate the Flood as a closed event, or
- treat New Testament confrontations as rhetorical exaggeration.

**Instead, read for:**

- how names, lineages, and authority structures persist,
- how corruption reappears in institutional and religious form, and
- how Scripture preserves memory across Testaments.

Chapter 11 must be read as a bridge text between Genesis and the Gospels.

**Teaching Explanation**

This chapter trains the student to recognize that judgment restrains corruption without yet concluding the conflict.

**As the student reads, observe how Scripture distinguishes between:**

- forgiveness (which restores relationship), and
- judgment (which preserves creation when corruption becomes structural).

**Chapter 11 requires attention to how post-Flood history includes:**

- resurfacing lineages,
- inherited authority systems, and
- religious structures that appear legitimate while carrying corrupted origin.

This explains why Yahusha and Yôchânân do not address the Second Temple leadership merely as mistaken or immoral, but as a generation—a term that signals origin, inheritance, and continuity.

**Alignment Focus of Chapter 11 (The Origin of Evil)**

While reading Chapter 11, the student must preserve the following controls:

- The Flood judged biological and structural corruption, not moral weakness alone
- Remnant corruption persists through bloodlines, names, lineage, and authority, not chaos
- Second Temple leadership reflects usurped continuity, not covenant fidelity
- Confrontation language in the Gospels is genealogical and juridical, not rhetorical insult
- Judgment restrains corruption while awaiting final resolution
- Chapter 11 preserves Scriptural coherence by demonstrating that Genesis categories remain operative in the apostolic era.

## KEY TERMS WEEK 27

- Flood: global judgment designed to cleanse creation from irreversible corruption
- Containment: divine restraint that limits spread while postponing final eradication
- Remnant Corruption: residual lineage or influence that survives judgment
- Genealogical Confrontation: addressing origin rather than behavior alone

# COVENANTAL STUDY TASK

*Pause your reading and engage the assigned texts directly:*

- **Explain why forgiveness alone could not address pre-Flood corruption.**
- **Identify at least two Scriptural indicators of post-Flood remnant corruption.**
- **Demonstrate how Yahusha's and Yôchânân's language targets lineage and origin, not isolated acts.**

Write analytically, not devotionally.

## FINAL THOUGHTS

Week 27 disciplines the student against sentimental readings of mercy. Scripture presents judgment and mercy as complementary, not contradictory.

The Flood did not fail.

It preserved creation by restraining corruption until redemption could confront it fully in history.

## QUOTE REFLECTION

"Preservation is not indulgence; restraint is not cruelty."

Reflect on how judgment protects creation where mercy alone cannot restore order.

*TERM II · MONTH 3 — WEEK 28*
# AFTER THE FLOOD
The Return of Corruption

**Learning Outcomes**

By the end of this week, the student will be able to:

- Explain why post-Flood corruption reappears without contradicting judgment
- Distinguish physical hybridization from spiritual and institutional continuation
- Identify how demonic activity operates under altered post-judgment conditions
- Demonstrate that New Testament confrontations presume ongoing corruption, not anomaly
- Preserve covenant accountability while recognizing demonic persistence under restraint

**Purpose of Week 28**

Week 28 addresses a Yada Yahuah tension that arises naturally after the Flood: If judgment cleansed the earth, why does corruption reappear in later Scripture—especially in the New Testament?

Chapter 12 answers this question by requiring the student to abandon the assumption that judgment equals total eradication. The Flood restrained corruption at the level of flesh, but Scripture testifies that rebellion re-emerges under new forms.

The purpose of this week is to train the student to recognize that post-Flood corruption continues through surviving Nephilim lineage, spirits, doctrines, and systems, rather than through new large-scale hybridization.

## TERM II - MONTH 3 - WEEK 28 - READING

Read Chapter 12 with attention to mode of operation, not escalation.

**The student must resist readings that:**

- assume demonic activity indicates failure of judgment, or
- collapse New Testament encounters into metaphor or formation.

**Instead, read for:**

- how corruption adapts after restraint,
- how authority and limitation are maintained, and
- how Scripture categorizes activity without exaggerating power.

Chapter 12 must be read as a post-judgment operational map, not a catalog of threats.

### Teaching Explanation

This chapter trains the student to recognize structural change without doctrinal change.

### After the Flood:

corruption no longer advances primarily through embodied hybridization, but through disembodied spirits, false instruction, and institutionalized idolatry.

The student must observe how Scripture consistently presents these spirits as:

- identifiable,
- confrontable, and
- subordinate to divine authority.

Equally important is recognizing that systems—religious, economic, and ideological—can function as containers for demonic influence, allowing corruption to persist culturally even where overt rebellion is restrained.

### Alignment Focus with Chapter 12 (The Origin of Evil)

While reading Chapter 12, the student must preserve the following distinctions:

- Judgment restrains method, not moral responsibility
- Demonic activity continues under limitation, not autonomy
- Possession, disease, and deception replace physical hybridization
- Idolatry disguises itself as culture, economy, or ideology
- Covenant obedience remains the decisive boundary

Chapter 12 does not reintroduce pre-Flood conditions; it explains how corruption survives after judgment without violating order.

## KEY TERMS WEEK 28

- Post-Flood Corruption: reemergence of disorder through bloodline, spirits, deception, and systems
- Demonic Spirits: disembodied remnants operating through influence rather than flesh
- Idolatry: worship of demons disguised as gods, ideologies, or institutions
- Containment: divine restraint that limits spread while preserving agency
- Reemergence: return of rebellion under new forms after judgment

# COVENANTAL STUDY TASK

*Engage the Scriptural witnesses directly and respond analytically:*

- ***Identify Scriptural evidence that demonic activity continues after the Flood under altered conditions.***
- ***Explain how post-Flood corruption differs structurally from pre-Flood hybridization.***

Do not summarize episodes. Analyze patterns, limits, and covenant responses.

## FINAL THOUGHTS

Week 28 disciplines the student against assuming that judgment eliminates vigilance.

The Flood proved that Yahuah intervenes when corruption threatens creation.

The New Testament proves that discernment, obedience, and covenant boundaries remain necessary afterward.

Judgment restrains evil; faithfulness prevents its return.

## QUOTE REFLECTION

"Restoration requires boundaries to remain intact."

Reflect on how covenant boundaries preserve restoration in

a restrained but contested world.

# TERM II · MONTH 3 — REINFORCEMENT TO DO (WEEKS 25–28)
## PURPOSE

This section reinforces the core foundations of Month 3.
If any principle below is unclear, the student must return to the corresponding week before proceeding.

- **Boundaries and Kinds Are Divine Design (Week 25)**
  Creation is ordered "according to kinds" as a deliberate act of divine separation
  Mixing that violates divinely assigned limits is treated as corruption, not diversity
- **Nephilim Are Historical and Continuous (Week 26)**
  Nephilim identity is grounded in Scriptural testimony and assigned canonical witnesses
- Post-Flood giant clans demonstrate continuity of abnormal lineages rather than isolated anomalies
- **The Flood Was Preservation Through Containment (Week 27)**
  The Flood addresses irreversible corruption that forgiveness alone cannot resolve
- Judgment restrains corruption but does not conclude the heavenly conflict
- **Corruption Reemerges After Judgment (Week 28)**
  Post-Flood corruption persists through spirits, deception, idolatry, and systemic influence
  Discernment and obedience remain required after containment is enacted

**Cumulative Month 3 Master Principle**

Hybridization violates divine boundaries, produces Nephilim corruption in flesh, and necessitates containment judgment; after containment, corruption reemerges through bloodline, spirits and systems until final judgment.

**Mandatory Student Action (Before Month 4)**

- Re-read any week where conceptual clarity is lacking
- Preserve Scriptural categories: kinds, boundary, hybridization, corruption, containment
- Do not collapse judgment into moral evil or emotional reaction

## TERM II – MONTH 4

**Academic Orientation — Term II · Month 4**

Term II · Month 4 completes The Origin of Evil and serves as the final instructional and evaluative phase of Stage II (Bachelor-Level Formation). This month is designed to move students from structured doctrinal acquisition into disciplined synthesis, culminating in a single integrative qualification submission at the end of the month.

Unlike previous months, Month 4 emphasizes application, tracing, and integration rather than the introduction of new doctrinal categories. Instruction continues through Weeks 29–31, where students engage with the final chapters of The Origin of Evil, followed by formal qualification assessment in Week 32.

**This module assumes demonstrated mastery of Term II · Months 1–3, especially:**

- Yahuah is not the source of moral evil
- Judgment functions as containment and preservation
- Corruption enters creation through boundary violation and hybridization
- Evil persists after judgment through spirits, systems, and Babel-pattern deception

**Student Expectations — Month 4**

Throughout Weeks 29–31, students are expected to:

- Integrate the full Term II framework without doctrinal contradiction
- Trace evil's persistence after judgment by agency, mechanism, and fruit

- Explain Babel as an organized, trans-historical system rather than isolated history
- Apply covenant language and canonical discipline independently
- Prepare for a final synthesis governed strictly by Scripture

Assertions must be supported by the assigned Scriptural witnesses and governed by covenantal reasoning, not philosophical speculation or inherited Yada Yahuah systems.

## MODULE OVERVIEW

### *Completion of The Origin of Evil & Bachelor-Level Synthesis*
*(Chapters 13–15)*

Month 4 completes The Origin of Evil by addressing what remains after judgment has already occurred. The focus shifts from how corruption entered to how corruption persists, examining the transformation of rebellion from physical hybridization into disembodied influence, centralized systems, and institutional deception.

**Weeks 29–31 provide structured instruction and guided analysis on:**
Disembodied corruption after physical judgment
- Babel as centralized, organized rebellion
- Ongoing deception as the primary weapon of evil
- Why judgment restrains corruption without erasing free will

Week 32 functions as the **formal qualification review,** where the student must demonstrate coherent integration of **Term II · Months 1–3**, governed by Month 4 synthesis.
Month 4 therefore tests **mastery and stability**, not memorization.

### Methodological Continuity — Synthesis & Qualification Standards

Month 4 continues the Scripture-first methodology of Term II and applies it with **qualification-level rigor.** All work in Weeks 29–32 is governe governed by the following principles:

- **Scripture Governs Conclusions**
  All claims must arise from Scriptural testimony and assigned witnesses, not tradition, philosophy, or institutional Yada Yahuah.
- **Terminology Remains Fixed**
  Key terms established in Months 1–3 (evil, corruption, rebellion, judgment, containment, deception, hybridization, Nephilim, Babel) may not be redefined, softened, or merged.
- **Agency Must Be Traced**
  Students must identify who acts, how evil operates, and by what mechanism (bloodline, spirits, systems, deception), avoiding abstraction and moral generalities.
- **Judgment Is Interpreted as Containment**
  Judgment is consistently treated as measured restraint and preservation of creation—not moral evil, cruelty, or divine failure.
- **Integration Is Required**
  Month 4 requires the student to connect heavenly rebellion, hybridization, Flood judgment, post-judgment spirits, and Babel systems into one coherent Scriptural framework.

These principles govern all Weeks 29–31 instructional tasks and the Week 32 qualification submission.

## CHAPTER COVERAGE
### The Origin of Evil — Chapters 13–16
- Chapter 13 — Disembodied Corruption
- Chapter 14 — Babel and Centralized Rebellion
- Chapter 15 — Ongoing Deception After Judgment

## MODULE LEARNING OUTCOMES — TERM II · MONTH 4

**By the end of Term II · Month 4, the student should be able to:**

- Explain why evil persists after physical judgment using Scriptural categories of agency and restraint
- Demonstrate the role of disembodied Nephilim spirits in post-Flood corruption
- Identify Babel as organized, centralized rebellion from Berēshīth through Apokálypsis
- Trace deception as the primary operating mechanism of evil after containment
- Apply covenant language, canonical, and covenantal discipline independently
- Produce a coherent integrative explanation that preserves the character of Yahuah

*Mastery is demonstrated through accurate synthesis, disciplined terminology, and Covenantal Reasoning.*

Month 4 determines eligibility for **Stage III — Master-Level Studies**, with formal qualification assessed in Week 32 only.

# DISEMBODIED CORRUPTION IN HISTORY

From Babel to Empire: When Rebellion Loses Flesh but Gains Power

## LEARNING OUTCOMES

By completing Week 29, the student will be able to:

- Read Chapter 13 as an argument about continuity mechanisms, not as a catalog of accusations.
- Distinguish between embodied rebellion and institutionalized corruption.
- Evaluate how authority, time, and naming function as juridical instruments.
- Maintain covenantal responsibility while recognizing post-judgment persistence.

## PURPOSE OF WEEK 29

The purpose of Week 29 is to train interpretive discipline.

Chapter 13 is not assigned to convince, provoke, or sensationalize.

It is assigned to demonstrate how corruption adapts after restraint, shifting from visible embodiment to systemic operation.

The student's task is to observe form change, not to litigate every historical assertion.

## TERM II – MONTH 4 – WEEK 29 – READING FROM CHAPTER 13 (THE ORIGIN OF EVIL)

When reading Chapter 13, the student must apply the following controls:

- Do not read as devotional affirmation or polemic rebuttal.
- Do not isolate individual claims from the chapter's governing thesis.
- Read for structural logic, not evidentiary exhaustion.
- Observe how continuity is argued, not whether every example persuades.

The chapter functions as a theoretical model, not a historical footnote archive.

**Teaching Explanation**

**Chapter 13 advances a single controlling idea:**

Corruption can persist without embodiment by relocating itself into systems that govern worship, time, language, and legitimacy.

**The instructional focus is therefore mechanism, not personality:**

- Power migrates from bodies to administration.
- Control shifts from force to routine.
- Visibility gives way to normalization.

The student is taught to recognize how authority can carry rebellion without appearing lawless.

## Alignment Focus with Chapter 13 (The Origin of Evil)

Week 29 aligns with the book's broader framework by preserving:

- **Agency:** Humans remain responsible participants.
- **Sequence:** Judgment precedes institutional continuity.
- **Assignment:** Authority structures transmit influence but do not absolve choice.

No new doctrines are introduced; Chapter 13 is read strictly within established parameters.

## Key Terms Week 29

- **Disembodied Corruption:** Rebellion operating through systems rather than bodies.
- **Institutional Continuity:** Persistence of influence through law, ritual, and authority.
- **Rebranding:** Preservation of function under altered designation.
- **Calendar Authority:** Governance of worship through control of time.

# COVENANTAL STUDY TASK

*The student must demonstrate covenantal discernment by addressing:*
*•Why corruption becomes harder to identify after judgment.*
*•How institutional legitimacy can mask misalignment.*
*•Why control of time and worship rhythms functions*
*as allegiance formation.*
*•How divine righteousness is preserved*
*when restraint does not equal eradication.*

Responses must remain analytical and juridical.

## FINAL THOUGHTS

Week 29 establishes that absence of spectacle is not absence of power.

When rebellion embeds itself in law, tradition, and routine, it becomes inherited rather than imposed.

The danger is not chaos — it is normalization.

The student must therefore learn to read structures, not appearances.

## QUOTE REFLECTION

"Judgment removed unlawful flesh; it did not erase unlawful memory."

This statement is not a conclusion to defend.
It is a reading discipline governing how Chapter 13 is approached — ensuring that restraint is not mistaken for resolution, and continuity is not confused with divine failure.

# BABEL IN APOKÁLYPSIS
What Began with a Tower Ends with a Throne

## PURPOSE OF WEEK 30

Week 30 completes the long arc of rebellion traced from Berēshīth to Apokálypsis. Babel is no longer approached as an ancient city, metaphor, or discarded empire. Chapter 14 establishes Babel as a living, cumulative system—the final maturation of post-Flood rebellion.

What began as unified defiance at a tower becomes, at the end of the age, a global throne: religious, political, and economic—administered deception rather than chaotic violence. Babel's defining sin is not ignorance, but pornía: covenant betrayal presented as sacred authority.

**This week trains the student to recognize continuity:**

- One rebellion
- Many manifestations
- One final judgment

### Babel as a System, Not a Ruin

Chapter 14 makes explicit what Scripture has long implied: Babel survives by transformation, not endurance of stone.

### In Apokálypsis, Babel:

- Reigns over kings (Rev 17:18)
- Intoxicates nations (Rev 14:8; 18:3)
- Accumulates bloodguilt (Rev 17:6; 18:24)
- Operates through farmakía (Rev 18:23)
- Becomes the habitation of demons (Rev 18:2)

**This reveals a decisive shift in how rebellion functions:**

- Genesis 11 → unified human defiance by proximity
- Revelation 17–18 → unified global defiance by administration

Babel no longer needs a tower. It rules through law, worship, economy, and doctrine.

## Pornía: The Defining Crime of Babel

Chapter 14 insists that pornía is not a secondary moral failure. It is Babel's primary sin.

## Pornía in Apokálypsis means:

- Spiritual prostitution
- Covenant betrayal
- Idolatry disguised as righteousness

Babel does not persecute truth openly at first. She seduces nations into believing that false worship is covenant faithfulness. This is why the nations are described as drunk—their discernment is impaired, not absent.

Thus:

- False worship feels holy
- Idolatry feels ancient and authoritative
- Demonic systems feel "Christianized," "normalized," or "traditional"

This explains why Babel's influence is universal. She conquers not by armies, but by redefinition of devotion.

## Farmakía: Control Through Engineered Deception

Chapter 14 directly links Babel's power to farmakía (Rev 18:23).

## Farmakía is not limited to occult ritual. In its Scriptural function, it is:

- Manipulation of belief
- Engineered deception

- Control of populations through spiritual intoxication

**Farmakía explains how:**
- Nations are deceived, not merely misinformed
- Worship becomes compulsory
- Truth is criminalized
- Bloodguilt becomes systemic

Babel's merchants grow rich because deception is profitable. Religion becomes an industry; doctrine becomes a tool; conscience becomes regulated.
Bloodguilt and the Necessity of Judgment

Chapter 14 leaves no ambiguity regarding Babel's guilt.

**In Babel is found:**
- The blood of prophets
- The blood of saints
- The blood of all killed upon the earth (Rev 18:24)

This is juridical language. Babel is not destroyed because she is old, powerful, or influential. She is destroyed because she has absorbed and preserved every act of covenant violence since the beginning.

**In Apokálypsis 19:2, judgment is declared:**
"True and righteous."
This confirms the central thesis of Term II:
Judgment is not divine instability.
Judgment is covenantal necessity when corruption becomes total.

**The End Mirrors the Beginning**
Chapter 14 deliberately returns the reader to Berēshīth.
- Then: corruption filled the earth → water
- Now: corruption fills the earth again → fire

**The cause is the same:**

Rebellion preserved and matured.

The method differs because the system has changed:

- Flesh was judged before
- Thrones, systems, and worship are judged now

The pattern is consistent. Only the scale has expanded.

Teaching Integration with Chapter 14 *of (The Origin of Evil)*

**Week 30 confirms:**

- Babel is a trans-generational system
- Rebellion survives judgment through memory, doctrine, and administration
- Pornía is covenant betrayal, not moral excess
- Farmakía is engineered deception, not superstition
- Judgment is required because corruption becomes global, public, and entrenched

What began with a tower ends with a throne.

What began in one land ends ruling all lands.

## KEY TERMS AND DEFINITIONS (WEEK 30)

- Babel (System): The cumulative, trans-generational structure of rebellion that survives by transformation rather than by preserving physical empire. In Week 30, Babel is defined as an administered global order—religious, political, and economic—through which covenant betrayal is normalized and enforced.
- Throne (of Babel): The matured form of post-Flood rebellion in which defiance is no longer localized by proximity (tower), but institutionalized through governance, worship, economy, and doctrine. The throne represents centralized authority that rules by regulation and redefinition rather than chaotic violence.
- Administration (of Rebellion): The organized management of deception

through systems that govern belief, devotion, and social order. Administration is the mechanism by which rebellion becomes universal, scalable, and durable—able to outlive generations and survive judgment through continuity of structure.

- Pornía (πορνεία): Covenant betrayal presented as sacred legitimacy. In Apokálypsis, pornía is spiritual prostitution—false worship, idolatry, and alliance with illegitimate authority disguised as righteousness—by which nations are seduced into mistaking violation for faithfulness.

- Spiritual Intoxication: The condition in which discernment is impaired through sustained exposure to Babel's redefined devotion. Spiritual intoxication explains why nations are "drunk": not lacking truth entirely, but rendered unable to distinguish covenant obedience from sanctioned corruption.

- Farmakía (φαρμακεία): Engineered deception used to manipulate belief and control populations through regulated worship and managed conscience. In Week 30, farmakía is not restricted to occult ritual; it is the systemic practice of spiritual control through deception, coercion, and institutionalized falsehood.

- Bloodguilt: Juridical covenant liability accumulated through preserved violence against Yahuah's witnesses. In Week 30, bloodguilt is the consolidated record of persecution found "in Babel," including prophets, saints, and covenant faithful—demonstrating that the system carries responsibility for cumulative covenant bloodshed.

- Cumulative Corruption: Rebellion preserved and matured across time until it becomes global, public, and entrenched. Cumulative corruption describes the arc from Genesis defiance to end-of-age system, where corruption is no longer episodic but normalized and self-sustaining.

- Universal Defiance: The final stage of rebellion in which kings, nations, merchants, and religious structures are unified under Babel's redefinition of worship and authority. Universal defiance is not merely widespread sin, but coordinated covenant opposition through shared system.

- Judgment (Covenantal Necessity): Boundary enforcement required when corruption becomes total and publicly enthroned. In Week 30, judgment is not divine volatility; it is the necessary covenant act that ends an irreversible system when rebellion reaches full maturation.

# *COVENANTAL STUDY TASK*

*Pause your reading and complete the following before proceeding. Engage the Scriptural text directly. Do not summarize secondary opinions.*
- *Trace the continuity of rebellion from Babel to Apokálypsis*
- *Distinguish localized defiance from administered, systemic betrayal*

## FINAL THOUGHT – WEEK 30

"What rebellion could not preserve by flesh, it preserved by system."

The fall of Babel is not tragedy—it is deliverance.

The destruction of the throne is the restoration of creation.

*TERM II · MONTH 4 — WEEK 31*

# THE COMPLETE ARC OF CORRUPTION
From Heavenly Rebellion to Final Extermination

## PURPOSE OF WEEK 31

Week 31 functions as integration, not escalation.

Chapter 15 gathers every major thread established across The Origin of Evil and orders them into a single, continuous arc:

**origin → violation → hybridization → judgment → restraint → persistence → final removal.**

This week corrects the long-standing Yada Yahuah error that places the burden of world corruption solely on humanity. Scripture, read sequentially and covenantally, identifies a **distinct initiating rebellion, a non-human escalation,** and **a preserved system of deception that survives judgment until the appointed end.**

The goal of Week 31 is not persuasion, but **coherence:**
students must be able to trace evil without collapsing categories, confusing agents, or misattributing cause.

**Governing Scriptural Anchors (Chapter 15 from The Origin of Evil)**

- **Enoch 14:5** — irreversible judgment against the Watchers
- **Enoch 21:8–10** — permanent confinement, not temporary discipline
- **Enoch 54:6** — final judgment reserved for the appointed day
- **Jubilees 5:6, 10** — binding of Watchers and destruction of their offspring
- **Matthew 13:41–42** — end-of-age removal of all causes of corruption

These texts establish sequence, restraint, and finality without contradiction.

**Teaching Explanation**

Evil Does Not Originate in Humanity

Chapter 15 begins by dismantling the assumption that evil originates in human nature itself.

- The fall in Eden introduces deception and disobedience, not genetic corruption.
- Humanity sins, but humanity is not yet structurally corrupted.
- Evil at this stage is moral and relational, not systemic or biological.

This distinction is foundational. Without it, every later judgment appears excessive or unjust.

## The Watcher Rebellion as Escalation

The descent of the Watchers marks a categorical shift:

- Boundary violation replaces temptation.
- Hybridization replaces persuasion.
- Corruption enters flesh, not merely thought.

The Nephilim are not violent humans; they are unauthorized beings, lacking the ruaḥ of Yahuah and contaminating creation by their existence.

This is why their destruction is preservative rather than punitive.

## The Flood as Preservation, Not Condemnation

Chapter 15 clarifies the Flood's purpose with precision:

- Judgment falls on corrupted flesh, not on humanity as such.
- Noaḥ and his household are preserved because integrity remains.
- The Flood removes hybrid bodies but does not erase memory, knowledge, or spirits.

Yahuah's covenant after the Flood confirms restraint, not indulgence.

## Demons as Residual Corruption

The death of Nephilim bodies produces a new condition:

- Disembodied spirits without rest
- Parasitic, not creative
- Influential, not sovereign

Demons are not created beings of Yahuah; they are residue.

This explains post-Flood corruption without requiring new angelic descent.

Babel as Systemic Adaptation

After judgment, rebellion adapts.

## Babel represents:

- The reintroduction of forbidden knowledge
- The consolidation of power without covenant
- A renewed attempt to unify heaven and earth unlawfully

Dispersion restrains consolidation, but systems survive, carried through mixed bloodlines, lineages, priesthoods, and cultures.

## Continuity into Religious Authority

Chapter 15 traces how this corruption embeds itself:

- In hostile nations
- In false priesthoods
- In Second-Temple leadership confronted by Yahusha
- In imperial religion under Rome

The continuity of Babel is functional, not ethnic:

centralization, false worship, persecution, and suppression of divine authority.

## Yahusha as Decisive Confrontation

Yahusha does not merely forgive sin; He exposes lineage-rooted authority.

- His language targets origin, not behavior alone.
- His death fulfills the ancient enmity.
- His resurrection secures future removal, not immediate eradication.

The conflict is resolved legally; execution awaits the appointed time.

## Final Extermination Reserved for the End

Scripture consistently places total removal at the end of the age:

- Watchers are bound, not annihilated
- Demons are active, not reigning
- Babel is judged progressively, then destroyed completely

This preserves both justice and patience within covenant order.

**Alignment Focus — Chapter 15 (The Origin of Evil)**
By the end of Week 31, students must retain these conclusions:
- Evil originates in deception, not divine creation
- Hybridization marks escalation, not inevitability
- Judgment restrains corruption without erasing its memory
- Demons are residual effects, not ruling powers
- Babel is a recurring system, not a single city
- Final extermination is future, total, and righteous

**Key Terms (Week 31)**
- Hybrid Corruption — contamination of created order through unlawful union
- Residual Evil — persistence of corruption after judgment through spirits and systems
- Systemic Rebellion — organized deception embedded in authority structures
- Final Extermination — complete removal of corruption at the appointed end

# COVENANTAL STUDY TASK

*Using Scripture and Chapter 15 only:*

• *Trace corruption from Eden to the present without collapsing agents or stages.*

• *Explain why the Flood preserved humanity rather than condemned it.*

• *Demonstrate how Babel functions as systemic rebellion after judgment.*

• *Explain why final extermination is reserved for the end of the age.*

## Final Thoughts — Week 31

"The Flood restrained corruption; it did not erase its memory."

History does not repeat because judgment failed,

but because rebellion learned to survive without flesh.

The end will not repeat the beginning.

It will finish it.

## QUOTE REFLECTION

"What judgment restrains in time, truth will eliminate in eternity."

# TERM II · MONTH 4 — REQUIRED REINFORCEMENT (TO BE COMPLETED BEFORE WEEK 32)
## PURPOSE

This section reinforces the core doctrinal framework of Month 4.

If any principle below remains unclear, the student must return to the corresponding week before proceeding to the final submission.

Month 4 addresses the persistence of evil after physical judgment, explaining why corruption continues through disembodied spirits, deception, and centralized systems, culminating in Babel's final exposure.

This reinforcement is mandatory review, not new teaching.

**Corruption Continues After Physical Judgment**

*(Week 29)*

- The Flood removed corrupted flesh, not the memory, influence, or will of rebellion
- Disembodied Nephilim spirits remain active as unclean spirits
- Evil relocates from biological corruption to spiritual and systemic influence
- Judgment restrains corruption without eliminating human responsibility

**Imperial Religion as Institutionalized Deception**

*(Week 30)*

- Babylonian worship persists under renamed forms and altered Yada Yahuah
- Roman imperial religion preserves pagan systems beneath sacred language
- Alteration of names, calendar, feasts, and worship practices embeds deception
- Constantine represents the transition from physical corruption to institutional control

## Babel as Centralized Global Rebellion

*(Week 31)*

- Babel is a continuing system, not a historical ruin
- Centralized authority replaces hybrid flesh as the vehicle of rebellion
- Religious, political, and economic power unify against Yahuah
- Babel is identified as the habitation of demons and the mother of deception

## Deception Explains the Persistence of Evil

*(Framework Confirmed Before Week 32)*

- Judgment restrains but does not reprogram free will
- Watchers are bound; Nephilim bodies destroyed; demons remain active
- Deception operates through doctrine, worship, systems, and belief
- Final judgment is reserved for fire, not water

## Cumulative Month 4 Master Principle

**Judgment restrains corruption without eliminating deception.**

After physical judgment, rebellion persists through **mixed bloodlines, disembodied spirits, altered worship, and centralized systems** until final judgment eradicates all corruption.

# FINAL QUALIFICATION & CAPSTONE SUBMISSION

Stage II (Bachelor-Level Formation)

## Academic Function of Week 32

Week 32 contains no new instructional material.

It serves exclusively as the formal qualification checkpoint concluding Term II — The Origin of Evil.

All doctrinal instruction is complete at the end of Week 31.

Week 32 evaluates whether the student can integrate, articulate, and apply the full Term II framework with academic discipline and Scriptural fidelity.

## Mandatory Student Preparation (Before Submission)

Before submitting the capstone paper, the student is expected to:

- Re-examine any prior week where conceptual uncertainty remains
- Preserve Scriptural categories precisely: judgment, deception, spirits, systems, agency
- Avoid attributing the persistence of evil to divine failure
- Avoid collapsing restraint into eradication
- Trace corruption by agency and fruit, not assumption or tradition

This preparation is student-directed and presumes full engagement with Weeks 17–31.

## Assessment Alignment — Term II · Month 4 (Summary)

The Month 4 sequence establishes the final analytical framework evaluated in Week 32:

- Week 29 — Post-Flood corruption through disembodied spirits
- Week 30 — Institutionalized deception through imperial and religious systems
- Week 31 — Babel as a global, centralized rebellion structure
- Week 32 — Demonstration that judgment restrains evil without eliminating deception

The student must integrate spiritual agency, deception, and containment into a single, coherent Scriptural explanation that preserves the righteousness of Yahuah.

**Final Submission Requirement (Mandatory)**
**Bachelor-Level Capstone Paper**
**Length:** 2,000–2,500 words
**Submission:** One paper only
Evaluation Basis: Scriptural reasoning and methodological consistency
Purpose
This paper is the sole integrative assessment for Term II. It evaluates the student's ability to explain the origin, mechanism, persistence, and restraint of evil using Scripture alone, without philosophical, denominational, or speculative frameworks.

**Required Focus Areas**
The paper must demonstrate mastery of all five areas below:

**Origin of Evil**
- Heavenly rebellion
- Boundary violation
- Distinction between corruption and moral evil

**Mechanism of Corruption**
- Hybridization
- Nephilim as a real Scriptural category
- Forbidden knowledge

**Judgment and Preservation**
- The Flood as preservative judgment
- Why forgiveness alone was insufficient
- Post-Judgment Persistence

- Disembodied spirits
- Babel as organized rebellion
- Ongoing deception

## Yada Yahuah Consequences
- Why traditional Yada Yahuah fails without Watchers
- Why evil does not originate in Yahuah
- Why final removal of evil is future-oriented

## Required Scriptures (Minimum)
The following texts must be meaningfully integrated, not merely cited:
- Berēshīth (Genesis) 3:1–6
- Berēshīth (Genesis) 6:1–4
- Berēshīth (Genesis) 6:11–13
- Berēshīth (Genesis) 10:8–12
- Berēshīth (Genesis) 11:1–9
- Deuteronomy 32:17
- Psalm 106:37–38
- Enoch 6–10 (selected passages)
- Enoch 15:8–12
- Matthew 12:43–45
- Revelation 17–18 (selected passages)

## Submission Standards
All submissions must comply strictly with the following:
- Scripture governs conclusions
- Clear structure and logical progression
- No devotional or sermonic language
- No denominational or philosophical systems
- No speculative Yada Yahuah
- Terminology must match definitions established in Months 1–3
- Covenantal Reasoning is required

The goal is demonstrated understanding, not persuasion.

## Qualification Threshold — Evaluation Criteria

Month 4, Week 32 evaluates competency, not participation.

### Satisfactory Performance Includes:

- Accurate Scriptural reasoning
- Faithful application of the restored Yada Yahuah method
- Correct distinction between evil, corruption, rebellion, and judgment
- Coherent integration of Term II (Months 1–3)
- Covenant language and doctrinal consistency
- Full compliance with methodological restrictions

### Unsatisfactory Performance Includes:

- Philosophical or metaphorical reduction
- Doctrinal contradiction or inconsistency
- Methodological deviation
- Redefinition of established terms
- Vague or imprecise language
- Failure to integrate the complete Term II framework

### Advancement Decision

At the conclusion of Week 32, faculty will issue one of the following determinations:

- Satisfactory — Bachelor-Level Equivalent Completed
- Unsatisfactory — Remediation Required

Only students receiving Satisfactory are eligible to proceed to:

## STAGE III — MASTER-LEVEL STUDIES

Failure to submit the capstone paper results in automatic disqualification from advancement.

Program Status Confirmation
Yahuah Institute of Biblical Restoration, Inc.

## STAGE II — BACHELOR-LEVEL FORMATION

Status: Completed upon satisfactory evaluation
Confirmed competencies include:

- Doctrine of evil and corruption
- Canonical and heavenly reasoning
- Scriptural judgment and preservation
- Nephilim and hybridization doctrine
- Babel and ongoing deception
- Academic Yada Yahuah discipline

**Final Notice to Students**

The structure is intentionally explicit:

- Month 4 is a qualification month
- Week 32 contains the single capstone submission
- The paper evaluates Months 1–3 only
- Scripture use is required, not suggested
- Methodological deviation results in disqualification
- Advancement is not automatic

**End of Term II — Bachelor-Level Qualification Complete**
Completion of Week 32 signifies fulfillment of Stage II — Bachelor-Level Formation.
Advancement to Stage III is contingent upon formal approval.
**No student may proceed without authorization.**

# CONCLUSION — BOOK 2 ⇸ BOOK 3

**Transition to MBRS Book 3 — Master-Level Foundations**

The second stage of the Master of Biblical Restoration Studies has carried the student beyond foundational authority into disciplined doctrinal formation. Evil has been defined according to Scripture alone. Corruption has been traced through rebellion and boundary violation. Judgment has been restored to its proper place as containment and preservation rather than moral accusation against Yahuah. Agency has been clarified, deception has been exposed, and covenant language has been refined.

At this point, the student no longer approaches Scripture through inherited Yada Yahuah assumptions, philosophical speculation, or theological tradition. Categories have been restored. Sequence has been established. The moral order of creation has been re-aligned with Scriptural testimony.
Yet doctrinal formation is not the final objective.

Having established correct categories, agency, and covenant logic, the student must now advance to Master-Level foundational study — where heavenly administration, covenant governance, priestly order, and restoration structures are examined in depth. The next stage moves from identifying corruption to understanding how Yahuah orders restoration across history, covenant, and kingdom.

MBRS Book 3 therefore transitions the student from Bachelor-Level doctrinal formation into Master-Level foundational administration — where restored knowledge becomes structured governance.

# TERM II — GLOSSARY

Administration: refers to the authorized ordering, stewardship, and execution of divine instruction, carried out through covenant-appointed priesthood. True administration exists to preserve, teach, and apply Yahuah's Tôrâh faithfully, without alteration, mixture, or innovation. Administration becomes corrupt only when it departs from authorization.

Adoption (Scriptural): The act of placement into a new spiritual lineage through transformation, not legal reclassification of unchanged nature.

Angels of the Presence: Heavenly beings associated with standing before Yahuah and involved in the transmission, witnessing, or declaration of divine instruction according to Scriptural testimony.

Ark of the Covenant: A sacred vessel designated to house the tablets of testimony, representing the authoritative witness of Yahuah's covenant. The Ark served as a focal point of divine presence, covenant accountability, and remembrance within Yâshâral's worship and instruction.

Authority: Delegated right to act under divine commission, accountable to heaven.

Authority vs. Influence – Authority is delegated right to command and govern within assigned bounds, while influence is the ability to persuade without lawful mandate or jurisdiction.

Author of the Earthly Tablets: Yahuah in origin, though delivered through appointed servants. While humans may transmit the tablets, authorship remains divine.

Birth (Covenantal): Establishment of new origin by divine initiation.

Calling: Yahuah's initiation of covenant identity.

Calendar Authority: refers to the governance of worship through control of appointed times as established by Yahuah in Scripture. The only legitimate calendar and authority over time is that which originates with Yahuah and is recorded in the Scriptural witness. Humanity does not possess the authority to alter, redefine, or legislate sacred time. Human attempts to modify or replace the Scriptural calendar—whether through tradition, institutional power, or political decree—constitute usurpation, not authorization, and result in distortion of worship rather than legitimate governance.

Conflict: The inevitable confrontation between Ruach-bearing humanity and flesh-only corruption.

Continuity: Sustained transmission of instruction and identity.

Continuity of Meaning: The faithful preservation of covenant doctrine through language, in which key terms retain their intended meaning across generations, writings, and administrations without contradiction.

Covenant Alignment: The state of being ordered rightly under Yahuah's commands, purposes, and assigned roles within the covenant structure.

Covenant Authorization: The explicit divine permission that legitimizes action within a defined role, office, or assignment.

Covenant Fulfillment: Completion of covenant purpose without cancellation or substitution.

Covenant Hope: The sustained expectation of restoration, vindication, and renewal grounded in Yahuah's covenant promises, preserved across generations through faithful instruction and confirmed through historical and prophetic witness.

Covenant Language: Scripturally governed vocabulary that preserves correct attribution and responsibility.

Covenant Language Unity: The consistent use and preservation of covenant vocabulary across Scriptural writings, ensuring that core theological meanings remain unified rather than fragmented by time, language, or context.

Covenantal Bridge: A preserved Scriptural witness that links earlier covenant expectation with later fulfillment, demonstrating continuity of divine purpose across time rather than theological rupture. A Covenantal Bridge shows how promise, pattern, and instruction are carried forward into fulfillment.

Custodian: A person or group entrusted with the responsibility to keep, protect, preserve, and faithfully transmit something of value. In this module, a custodian refers to those appointed to steward Dabar Yahuah without alteration, addition, or corruption.

Dabar (דָּבָר): The authoritative Word, command, decree, or instruction issued by Yahuah. In this Institute, Dabar refers to the expressed will of Yahuah through which creation was spoken, commandments were given, and truth is established.

Dabar Yahuah: The totality of Yahuah's authoritative instruction, including His commandments, decrees, testimonies, and revelations. Dabar Yahuah originates with Yahuah alone and stands as the supreme authority over humanity, Yada Yahuah, and doctrine.

Decalogue: The ten foundational commandments delivered in covenant context, representing a central expression of Yahuah's moral and covenantal instruction.

Delegated Judgment: Judgment carried out by authorized agents rather than by Yahuah directly

Discernment by Fruit – The evaluation of legitimacy and alignment based on observable outcomes rather than claimed authority or intention.

Doctrinal Continuity: The faithful transmission of covenant belief and instruction across time without contradiction, demonstrating consistency of divine purpose despite changes in administration, historical context, or mode of revelation.

Doctrines of Men: Teachings created or reshaped by human authority that replace, reinterpret, or nullify the commandments of Yahuah. Yahusha explicitly condemns such doctrines when they override divine instruction.

Earthly Tablets: The physical manifestation or copy of divine instruction delivered to humanity.

Earthly Tablets serve as a faithful transmission of what is first established in heaven.

Empowerment: Temporary Spirit enablement for function without nature replacement.

Faith: Covenantal trust in Yahuah that results in loyalty, obedience, and perseverance, demonstrated through faithful action rather than mere belief or verbal confession.

Faithful Priesthood: Priestly service that remains aligned with covenant instruction through obedience, integrity, and faithfulness to divine command. A faithful priesthood preserves authority by upholding Tôrâh, regardless of changing administrations or historical pressure.

Formation: Shaping of the Third Humanity toward purpose through internal renewal.

Fruit: The observable outcome that reveals origin and nature rather than effort or intention. Good fruit is the visible verification of Spirit-origin life aligned with Yahuah's instruction, flowing naturally from restored nature. Bad fruit is the manifestation of evil or corrupted nature, produced by disalignment, deception, or spiritual influence contrary to Yahuah's Tôrâh. Fruit therefore functions as a covenantal measure, exposing whether a life, teaching, system, or authority proceeds from the Ruach of Yahuah or from corrupted origin. It does not create legitimacy; it reveals it.

Grace: The unearned favor and active intervention of Elohiym that initiates rescue, sustains restoration, and empowers covenant faithfulness, rather than excusing disobedience or nullifying instruction.

Guardian: One who actively defends and safeguards what has been entrusted. A guardian not only preserves Scripture but also protects it from distortion, ensuring that Dabar Yahuah remains intact in teaching, transmission, and practice.

Harvest: The structural moment when coexistence ends and distinction becomes necessary.

Heavenly Tablets: The heavenly record in which Yahuah's decrees, appointed times, and judgments are established and preserved. In this Institute, Heavenly Tablets represent the original and incorruptible source of divine instruction.

High Priest: The chief priest within the priestly order, bearing the highest covenantal responsibility for intercession, sacred service oversight, and guardianship of holy instruction. In this module, the High Priest represents authorized spiritual governance tied directly to the preservation of Dabar Yahuah.

Indoctrination: The process by which belief is shaped and controlled by human systems rather than by direct engagement with Dabar Yahuah. Indoctrination replaces discernment with conformity.

Inheritance: That which is lawfully received by assignment or promise, rather than seized by desire or force. The transmission of nature and spiritual capacity through lineage. Covenant occupancy requiring alignment, not merely forgiveness.

Internalized Instruction: Divine law embedded through regenerated desire.

Jurisdiction: The defined sphere or boundary within which authority is legitimately exercised and outside of which action becomes transgressive. Authority determining ownership, allegiance, and identity.

Justice: Rightful alignment assessment applied universally, without exemption or bias.

Levitical Priesthood: Temporary covenantal system under Sinai

Light: Alignment with Yahuah's order, instruction, and covenantal authority.

Malkîy-Tsedeq: A priest-king figure presented in Scripture as representing a priesthood order not based on Levitical descent. In this module, Malkîy-Tsedeq introduces the concept of a higher, enduring priesthood, culminating in Yahusha ha Mashiyach as the ultimate covenantal High Priest.

Mercy: Yahuah's intentional safeguarding of His created order and covenant purpose before, during, and beyond judgment.

Mosaic Torah: The formal administration of Tôrâh delivered through Mosheh to Yâshâral. In this module, Mosaic Torah is understood as a codified transmission of instruction that already existed, not the origin of divine law.

Nephesh Chayah: Fleshly, breathing life introduced by Yahuah's command.

New Testament: The body of inspired writings documenting the life, teachings, death, resurrection, and covenantal fulfillment through Yahusha ha Mashiyach and His emissaries. In Institute context, these writings do not replace the Tôrâh but testify to its fulfillment.

Obedience: Alignment flowing naturally from restored nature.

Oath: A binding declaration that seals intent and removes retreat from transgression.

Patriarchal Line: A preserved sequence maintaining covenant alignment.

Pentateuch: The first five books traditionally attributed to Mosheh, containing creation accounts, covenant formation, instruction, and legal foundations. In Institute usage, the Pentateuch is part of a broader continuum of Tôrâh, not its origin.

Preparation: Intentional divine action established before crisis manifests.

Preservation: Yahuah's restraint of corruption until the appointed time. Intentional safeguarding of redemptive continuity prior to confrontation. Sustaining covenant identity through discipline and presence amid instability.

Priestly Continuity: The ongoing transmission of covenantal authority and responsibility from one appointed priestly administration to another, without interruption in divine instruction or purpose. Priestly continuity affirms that Yahuah's covenant order is maintained through faithful stewardship rather than terminated by historical change.

Priestly Guardianship: Covenant-appointed stewardship of Dabar Yahuah

Priesthood: The covenant-appointed order set apart to minister before Yahuah and to teach, preserve, and administer His Tôrâh among the people. Priesthood is not merely religious leadership; it is an authorized covenant office with defined responsibilities and boundaries.

Progression: Forward movement toward restoration, not reversal to innocence.

Prophetic Purpose: Foreknowledge embedded into history to guide preservation and judgment.

Public Reading: The communal proclamation of covenant instruction before the people, intended to restore understanding, renew obedience, and re-establish alignment with Yahuah's commands. Public reading functioned as both teaching and corrective restoration within the covenant community.

Purification: The removal of corrupted elements to preserve what remains viable within creation.

Purity: A textually preserved state of alignment identifiable through distinction and continuity.

Qadosh: Set apart by design, not achieved through recovery.

Regeneration: Creation of new origin through direct Spirit action.

Renewed Covenant: The covenantal fulfillment in which existing divine instruction is reaffirmed, internalized, and rightly applied through the Messiah, rather than abolished or replaced. The renewed covenant emphasizes restoration of obedience and understanding, not cancellation of Tôrâh.

Restraint: The intentional limitation of action in obedience to Yahuah's given boundaries and prohibitions. Limitation of corruption without elimination of agency. Refusal to adopt corrupt methods, even when confronting darkness.

Resurrection: The divinely enacted restoration of life following death, affirming that covenant faithfulness, obedience, and righteousness are not nullified by mortality but are preserved for future renewal and judgment according to Yahuah's purpose.

Revelation: The divinely timed unveiling of previously preserved truth, made known in accordance with covenant purpose and fulfillment rather than through innovation or alteration.

Righteous Sufferer: A faithful covenant servant who remains obedient amid persecution, injustice, or rejection, whose suffering serves as testimony rather than disqualification and is ultimately answered by divine vindication.

Salvation (Yāshaʿ / Sōtēría): The covenantal act of deliverance and restoration accomplished by Yahuah through Yahusha. Yāshaʿ (Hebrew) expresses rescue, deliverance, and being brought into safety by divine intervention, while Sōtēría (Greek) emphasizes preservation, rescue, and restoration unto life. Salvation rescues the faithful from judgment and corruption and restores them to right standing, covenant identity, and purpose within the covenant established by Yahuah, rather than merely offering forgiveness detached from transformation or obedience.

Sanctification: Setting apart as holy, complete, and belonging to Yahuah.

Scriptures: The inspired written record of Dabar Yahuah transmitted to humanity through appointed means. In Institute usage, Scriptures are not merely religious texts, but documented divine instruction bound by covenantal authority.

Selective Revelation: Yahuah's intentional focus on what advances redemption.

Stewardship: Responsible governance exercised within Yahuah's established order. Responsible use of authority for protection, order, and covenant purpose.

Submission: Alignment with divine order—not inferiority, but rightful placement under heaven.

Tanakh (Old Testament): The body of inspired writings documenting creation, covenant, instruction, and prophetic testimony prior to the renewed covenant era. In Institute context, these writings form a foundational portion of Dabar Yahuah.

Temple: A covenantal appointed dwelling place where Yahuah's presence, instruction, and order were stewarded through priestly service. The Temple functioned as a center for teaching, preservation of sacred testimony, and regulated covenant life, rather than merely a physical structure.

Transitions of Priesthood: The divinely directed process by which covenantal priestly roles move from one administration to another in accordance with Yahuah's purpose, culminating in completion rather than disruption. Such transitions preserve continuity while bringing the covenant order to its intended fullness.

Two Conditions: The distinction between obedience and transgression, under which all covenant actions and outcomes are evaluated.

Walk: The visible expression of restored origin, not a method of transformation.

Witness: Visible testimony of restored humanity expressed through light-filled living.

Yada Yahuah: Restored knowledge derived from Scriptural order, covenantal structure, and lawful sequence. The covenantal act of knowing Yahuah through His self-revelation, instruction, and lived obedience. It is not speculative reasoning about Elohiym, but relational knowing grounded in faithfulness, encounter, and submission to His Word.

Yahusha: The biblical Hebrew Name of the Messiah, preserved in Scripture and composed of two covenantal elements: Yahu (bearing the Name of the Father, Yahuah) and Yāshaʿ (to save or deliver). The Name Yahusha therefore means "Yahuah saves." It is not a modern construction or institutional restoration, but the true Scriptural Name revealing identity, mission, and authority. Yahusha ha Mashiyach is recognized as the fulfillment and perfect embodiment of Yahuah's Tôrâh and the ultimate authority who restores proper understanding of Dabar Yahuah. He is presented as the final and faithful High Priest, executing covenant fulfillment without abolishing or replacing divine instruction.

www.ingramcontent.com/pod-product-compliance
Lightning Source LLC
Chambersburg PA
CBHW080608090426

42735CB00017B/3365